Fiscal Federalism: A Comparative Introduction

George Anderson

Forum of Federations

OXFORD

UNIVERSITY PRESS

OXFORD
UNIVERSITY PRESS

8 Sampson Mews, Suite 204, Don Mills, Ontario M3C 2G7
www.oupcanada.com

Oxford University Press is a department of the University of Oxford.
It furthers the University's objective of excellence in research, scholarship, and education by publishing
worldwide in

Oxford   New York

Auckland   Cape Town   Dar es Salaam   Hong Kong   Karachi   Kuala Lumpur   Madrid
Melbourne   Mexico City   Nairobi   New Delhi   Shanghai   Taipei   Toronto

With offices in
Argentina   Austria   Brazil   Chile   Czech Republic   France   Greece   Guatemala
Hungary   Italy   Japan   Poland   Portugal   Singapore   South Korea   Switzerland
Thailand   Turkey   Ukraine   Vietnam

Oxford is a trade mark of Oxford University Press in the UK and in certain other countries

Published in Canada by Oxford University Press

Library and Archives Canada Cataloguing in Publication

Anderson, George, 1945–
Fiscal federalism : a comparative introduction /
George Anderson

ISBN 978-0-19543-238-1

1. Intergovernmental fiscal relations.   2. Intergovernmental tax relations.
3. Revenue sharing.   4. Fiscal policy.   5. Finance, Public.   I. Title.

HJ197 A53 2009   336.1'85   C2009-903690-8

2 3 4 5 - 13 12 11 10

This book is printed on permanent acid free paper ∞.
Printed and bound in Canada.

Table of Contents

Preface and Acknowledgements

Money is central to the life of federations, as it is for any form of democratic government. Federations have all the normal debates that other democracies do over money—whom and what to tax, how to spend, and whether to run surpluses or deficits. But federal debates have an added layer of complexity because there are at least two constitutionally established tiers of government, each with its own powers, responsibilities, and perspectives.

Debates around money are perennial in federations, and outcomes evolve with different parties in power, shifts in regional wealth, and changes in the prevailing wisdom. The dynamic and critical role of "fiscal federalism" makes it one of the most studied aspects of federalism. Federal constitutions are typically quite stable because special majorities are needed to change them. Financial arrangements, by contrast, are much less stable since shares and sources of revenues, the priorities of public spending, and government surpluses or deficits can shift dramatically in short periods. Moreover, fiscal arrangements in many federations have often trumped constitutional or political arrangements, in the sense that power has gone where the money is. It is natural that fiscal issues are so often at the heart of political debates in federations.

There is a whole school of professional scholars who study fiscal federalism, but their writing is often quite inaccessible to intelligent lay readers, who conclude the subject is too complex for them to understand. It is not. This little book is designed to provide politicians, officials, citizens, and students with a concise and non-technical overview of fiscal federalism, drawing on the relevant work of economists and political scientists. It is practical in tone and it uses everyday, non-specialist language.

This book complements my similar volume, *Federalism: An Introduction*. Readers will find the non-fiscal dimensions of federalism more fully set out there. This book has seven chapters, each divided into five to nine sections, which start with a short capsule paragraph in bold type giving the essential point of the section. This is then elaborated, sometimes with inset boxes illustrating the range of federal experiences or giving key case examples. Those interested in further reading can refer to the section at the end of this volume. The Forum of Federations' website (www.forumfed.org) also provides important source references by chapter and a fuller bibliography.

As with *Federalism: An Introduction* (which has been translated into many languages), this book will be used and "road tested" by the Forum of Federations in its work around the world. We would be grateful for comments or suggestions from readers that may help us improve future editions.

For such a small book, I have incurred a large number of debts.

First, I must thank Coel Kirkby who served as my research assistant over several months and largely prepared the bibliography and chapter references, as well as doing much fact chasing. Robin Boadway kindly agreed to act as an advisor and read an early outline in addition to two drafts, providing invaluable advice and knowledge at every step. Indira Rajaraman was originally to be the author and I worked closely with her on the first outline; her nomination to the Finance Commission of India took her to a higher calling, but even so she kindly reviewed the draft, especially on matters relating to India.

My Canadian colleagues Ron Watts, André Plourde, David Peloquin, and Anwar Shah (at the World Bank) all did careful readings of the whole manuscript and made many useful suggestions. A large number of colleagues in other countries either read it and provided helpful comments, or contributed to my understanding by answering questions about the sometimes arcane arrangements and politics in their countries: Miguel Angel Asensio and Juan Antonio Zapata in Argentina; Michael Crommelin in Australia; Fernado Rezende in Brazil; Henrik Scheller in Germany; Ligia Noronha in India; Wee Chong Hui in Malaysia; Victor Carreon in Mexico; Rotimi Suberu in

Nigeria; Gulfaraz Ahmed in Pakistan; Galina Kurlyandskaya and Michel Subotin in Russia; Maite Vilalta and Carles Viver in Spain; Peter Mieszkowski and Ron Soligo in the United States; and Osmel Manzano in Venezuela. I gained many insights on matters large and small from several of these individuals at an authors' workshop sponsored by the Forum of Federations on oil and gas in federations. A comparative volume on that subject is forthcoming.

I have also benefited from excellent support from Rod Macdonell at the Forum and David Stover at Oxford University Press. Marta Tomins did her usual superb job of copy editing. Of course, I alone am responsible for any remaining errors.

George Anderson,
President and CEO,
Forum of Federations

Chapter One

An Overview of Fiscal Federalism

1.1 Political federalism

Federalism is a constitutionally established system with at least two orders of government each of which has some genuine autonomy from the other. The governments at each level are primarily accountable to their respective electorates.

There are over two dozen countries that call themselves federal or are usually considered to be so. They are home to about 40 percent of the world's people. Typically, democracies with very large territories (Canada, USA, Brazil, Australia) and very large populations (India, Pakistan, Nigeria) are federal. So are some small countries with very diverse populations (Switzerland, Belgium, Bosnia and Herzegovina), and some island states (Comoros, Micronesia, St. Kitts and Nevis). Some federations trace their federal origins back to the eighteenth (United States) or nineteenth centuries (Canada, Switzerland, Germany, Austria), while others are much more recent (Malaysia, Spain, South Africa, Ethiopia) or still in the process of becoming (Iraq, Sudan).

These countries and their political systems are extremely varied. The essence of being federal is having at least two constitutionally established orders of government—typically a **federal** government and **constituent-unit** governments (frequently called states or provinces, but also cantons, Länder, communities, islands and other names)— each of which has some genuine, constitutionally based autonomy and a direct electoral relationship with its population. In a few federations (Brazil, India, Nigeria, South Africa), the municipal or local order of government is also established within the constitution.

(Confederations, by contrast, have central governments formed by the member states, not elected directly. The European Union is a unique combination of confederal, federal, and treaty arrangements.) Some countries considered to be federal (Spain, South Africa) may not use the term for themselves. Given the fundamental role of constitutions in federations, the rule of law and democracy are a normal feature of federations, although some countries that claim to be federal may fail on both counts. Federations are extremely varied in their form and functioning, covering a wide range from very decentralized to highly centralized.

1.2 *Fiscal federalism*

Fiscal federalism studies the respective roles and interaction of governments within federal systems, with a particular focus on the raising, borrowing, and spending of revenues. It examines the functioning of these systems and tries to provide a principled basis for evaluating them. The study of fiscal federalism can also be relevant for the fiscal arrangements in devolved systems of government that are not strictly federal.

While the boundaries of fiscal federalism are hard to draw, the core of the subject is clearly the raising, borrowing, and spending of money in federations. It is a big subject that necessarily includes the means by which money is raised, the purposes for which it is spent, and the respective roles of federal and constituent governments in this process. It can be both explanatory and evaluative: how and why things happen; what would be an optimal or better way?

Take raising money, for example. Fiscal federalism may look at who has the authority to raise various kinds of taxes in a federation, but it can also consider whether to recommend a particular distribution of tax authorities. Does the allocation of taxing powers affect the actual tax policies adopted by one government or another? If so, is this in the public interest? Does the authority to raise money match expenditure responsibilities? Should rich regions be taxed to provide revenues for poorer regions? Which governments should have what rights to borrow money?

Similarly, the spending and sharing of revenues raises major issues. Do constituent units have adequate authority to raise their own revenues to meet their spending responsiblities? If not, what arrangments are in place for them to share taxes with, or receive transfers from, the federal government? Do federal transfers include conditions, and, if so, what do these imply for constituent-unit autonomy, program functioning, or policy coherence? Is spending by governments in the federation centralized or decentralized, and how might this affect relationships and policies?

Regulation, too, is important because both orders of government may make regulations that have economic implications; e.g., regarding financial institutions, labour markets, and trade in services and goods within a federation's internal market.

Fiscal federalism also looks at how decisions are made. Are fiscal decisions made separately, jointly, or cooperatively? Is the federation marked by major tensions or consensus around revenue raising and spending? Are there joint administrative arrangements for delivering programs or raising revenues? How do federal political and fiscal arrangements affect economic performance?

Of course, some **unitary** countries have also devolved significant spending and taxing powers to regional governments. While such devolution may not be constitutionally federal, it can be quite federal in practice. Thus questions of fiscal federalism can apply, for example, to the Nordic countries, China, and Japan—all of which have some decentralized fiscal features.

1.3 Institutional variety of federalism

Federations differ in their historic origins, the number of constituent units, their executive and legislative institutions, their electoral regimes and party systems, and their division of powers. The character of a federal fiscal regime is determined by the who, how, how much, and what for of revenue raising, sharing, and spending among governments. All of these factors can be important when considering fiscal arrangements within a federation.

While this book focuses on the federal fiscal arrangements, these are shaped by broader historical, institutional, political, and social contexts. Take the number of constituent units for example: there can be as few as two (the old Pakistan), or three (the original Nigeria), or as many as 83 (Russia), or 50 (the United States). Federations with very few units tend to be unstable and difficult to manage, while those with many constituent units may tend towards centralization and weak intergovernmental relations. Central institutions matter, too: cabinets in parliamentary regimes usually have more control over budgets than do presidents in congressional regimes; upper houses can have a key role—or no role—in budgetary matters; political parties can be highly disciplined or quite loose coalitions. All these factors will affect a federation's fiscal dynamics.

Federations differ greatly in the allocation of powers:

- Under the so-called classical or **dualist model** of federalism (as in Canada or the United States), each order of government normally administers its own laws through its own civil service, while in the **integrated model** of federalism (as in Germany, Switzerland, or Spain) the federal government passes many laws that the constituent units then administer.

- Some federations have many **concurrent** legislative powers, where each order of government can legislate on the same subject (but with federal law normally being paramount), while others tend to a clearer division of powers to one order of government or the other.

- In most federations, governments make their decisions on their own, but some provide for **joint decision-making by governments** (Germany, and to some extent South Africa and Ethiopia).

- The **allocation of specific powers** differs significantly between federations. Some are highly centralized and others are decentralized. Key taxing and economic powers can be assigned very differently across federations.

A federation where the federal government raises most revenues and finances constituent units through highly conditional transfers will be quite different from one where the constituent units are largely funded by taxes and borrowing that they decide for themselves. While some see only the latter model as being truly federal, federal practice and thinking includes both.

1.4 Fiscal arrangements and flexibility

While some basic fiscal arrangements, such as taxing powers, are typically set down in a federal constitution, many important features are not. Fiscal arrangements are usually more flexible than the basic division of legislative and administrative powers of the two orders of government. This flexibility means that fiscal arrangements are often central to political debates in federations.

Typically most of the defining features of a federation—the number of constituent units, its major institutions, the division of legislative and administrative powers—are set down in the constitution. These are usually hard to change because constitutional amendments normally require special majorities (though some federations permit powers to be delegated between orders of government). However, constitutions cannot specify many major fiscal features of a federation, such as how much is to be spent on what, what taxes are to be most important, and the specifics of fiscal transfers from the central to the constituent-unit governments. Such features must be worked through in day-to-day politics, which can be competitive as well as co-operative.

1.5 Evaluation of federal fiscal regimes

The study of fiscal federalism includes the evaluation of fiscal arrangements. Evaluative criteria include economic efficiency, equity, administrative simplicity, incentives for innovation, accountability, balancing responsibilities and means, predictability, and stability. Some criteria are conceptually difficult, and different criteria can conflict with one another. Many of these criteria apply equally to unitary regimes. There is no best model of fiscal federalism: a preferred choice will depend on the value and interpretation assigned to different criteria.

Economic efficiency is a central concern of economics. It focuses on using scarce resources in a non-wasteful manner. Fiscal federalism looks at different dimensions of economic efficiency:

- One is the efficiency of internal markets. In federations, different governments may create internal market distortions because of **policies that protect or favour local producers**, e.g., in procurement decisions, regulations, or the right to invest, and create barriers to the efficient flow of investments or labour among constituent units.

- Similarly, well-off constituent units may use their **fiscal advantage**, as opposed to their underlying competitive advantages, for low taxes and good services to attract investments and labour.

- Finally, federal arrangements can affect the efficient provision of public goods and services, including their **costs and benefits**, as well as **administrative simplicity**. Efficiency in this case includes considerations of economies of scale, of spillovers of costs and benefits across the borders of constituent units, and of the distinct preferences of different populations.

Equity or fairness is also central to many fiscal debates. The meaning of "equity" is not always clear, though it requires treating like cases alike and different cases with a fair measure of proportionality. In federal regimes, there are two aspects to this:

- First, equity both between the federal and constituent-unit governments, given their responsibilities (**vertical equity**), and among the constituent-unit governments, given their different means and needs (**horizontal equity**)

- Secondly, equity among citizens. Addressing disparities among citizens across a federation implies a more interventionist role for a central government than addressing disparities among governments. Putting the central government in a more direct role with citizens can draw it into areas where the constituent units may have major responsibilities.

Some believe equity should apply only among individuals, rather than among governments, which strengthens the argument for a regime's providing similar standards of public services in all constituent units.

Efficiency and equity can be in conflict or in harmony; for example, a view of equity that undermined rewards for hard work would also undermine the efficient operation of an economy. On the other hand, investments in the equitable provision of education, health care, and infrastructure in underdeveloped regions may build the wealth of a nation and prove efficient. We shall repeatedly encounter the issues of efficiency and equity because they pervade thinking on fiscal federalism (as on public policy more generally). These important concepts are not given to easy answers, and political opponents sometimes use the language of efficiency and equity to justify very different positions.

A central justification for federalism is that it permits a governmental system that is more **responsive**, in that different governments—federal and regional—can respond to the particular priorities of their populations. A further justification claimed for federalism is that it provides **incentives for innovation** because different governments can compete and try out alternative approaches and learn from one another. But the wrong types of competition can themselves create distortions.

Some evaluative criteria relate to the operating principles of a federation. These include the following:

- **Adequacy** of fiscal arrangements in finding a reasonable match between spending responsibilities and revenues or revenue powers (another way of thinking about vertical equity).

- **Predictability and stability**, particularly for constituent-unit governments that may depend heavily on federal support and have limited access to broad tax bases or debt markets.

- **Accountability**. Federal governments often raise funds that they transfer to constituent units. To whom should constituent units be accountable for these funds: the federal government, their own publics, or both?

Central governments in federations can have important powers in relation to constituent units—powers to disallow legislation, impose legal mandates, attach conditions to fiscal transfers, and even suspend constituent-unit governments. Such provisions are often criticized as non-federal or **quasi-federal**, but ultimately the choice regarding such arrangements is for each country to make, given its own priorities, values, and balance between national and sub-national communities. Federations such as Canada and India started with a number of quasi-federal aspects and moved over time in a more decentralized, classically federal direction, while other federations became more centralized.

It should be clear from this overview of criteria for evaluating fiscal regimes in federal contexts that there can be no single best arrangement, even for a particular federation.

Chapter Two

Expenditure Responsibilities

2.1 Expenditure patterns in governments

Over the past century, the relative size of government spending has grown hugely in advanced economies; it has also grown in developing countries, but typically to lower levels. Federalism seems to have little to do with this growth. The big spending programs are usually for social security and welfare, health, education, and defence. Modern governments provide public goods, as well as programs and services that benefit individuals, and such services can have strong elements of redistribution.

Big government is a fact of life in virtually all rich democracies. In some advanced economies, government spending accounts for over half of gross domestic product, while even in the lowest spending ones, it accounts for about one quarter of GDP. Federations can be found across the spectrum from high- to relatively lower-spending countries. Developing countries typically have smaller government spending as a share of GDP because much economic activity is outside the cash economy, and the revenue base for governments can be quite limited. Developing countries usually cannot afford the elaborate social safety nets and welfare programs of advanced economies. One area where governments have retreated in recent years is in the public ownership of corporations—such as utilities, financial insitutions, and resource and industrial companies—as many such enterprises have been sold to private interests.

Economic theory suggests governments should provide so-called **public goods**, such as defence and policing, which benefit the whole public because the free market would under-provide such goods.

Governments also provide such expensive programs as health care, education, social safety nets, welfare, and major infrastructure, which benefit both the public at large and the direct users of these programs, sometimes called **quasi-public goods**. Such programs often have a strongly **redistributive** element, from wealthier taxpayers to big consumers of the programs.

2.2 Principles of expenditure assignment

The literature on fiscal federalism has developed various principles for assigning expenditure responsibilities among governments. In practice, most constitutions assign legislative responsibilities explicitly and expenditure responsibilities only implicitly. Assignment principles include giving responsibility to the order of government whose population benefits from a public good, devolving program administration when there is a strong advantage in feedback from the population being served, and providing for some federal role in major programs that redistribute wealth among individuals. In many program areas there is a justification for both orders of government to be involved.

Constitutions usually assign legislative, not expenditure, responsibilities. The responsibility to administer spending programs normally flows from legislative responsibility. There are, however, exceptions, notably in integrated federations, such as Germany, where the constitution may stipulate that constituent-unit governments (or even local governments) will administer programs in areas of concurrent legislative responsibility.

The issue of how best to assign responsibilities in federations is linked to broader considerations about devolved forms of government. Arguments for devolution claim that it provides greater **public choice** because sub-national units of government are closer and more responsive to local populations, that multiple constituent-unit governments can act as policy laboratories and learn from one another, and that decentralization provides checks against an abusive concentration of power. However, those who emphasize the **welfare** of individual citizens and the need for coherent policies across a country often advocate more centralized government.

Whatever the general appetite for devolved government, the assignment of specific responsibilities to each order of government must be decided. In the early history of fiscal federalism as a subject, there was a strong emphasis on matching the population benefiting from a public good to the appropriate level of government as provider. For example, defence is a public good that clearly benefits the whole public of the country; local roads, by contrast, mainly benefit a small, geographically limited public. While the theory of public goods seems clear, its application in practice can be messy. Defence and local roads seem straightforward. But many public goods, such as policing, serve national and regional publics in different degrees, so it is hard to draw boundaries.

Moreover, the big spending areas of health care, education, pensions, unemployment insurance, and welfare further complicate the picture. For reasons of cost efficiency and local responsiveness their management may best be decentralized, but this may result in citizens across the country getting very different treatment and create barriers to mobility. Thus, for reasons of equity and program integrity, the central government should have a role. This is particularly true of some transfers to individuals, such as child transfers, pensions, and some transfers based on need, where there may be no particular advantage to delivery by constituent units. A balance may have to be found in which both orders of government share responsibility.

In practice, the main allocation of expenditure responsibility in most federations was decided with little reference to the theories of fiscal federalism. However, the principles can be useful for countries considering federal constitutions and established federations seeking to readjust responsibilities.

2.3 Integrated or dualist federal systems

In dualist federations, governments normally administer their own legislated programs, while, in integrated federations, the constituent units administer federal laws in specified areas. Many federations have elements of both models. Constituent units in integrated federations may have significant administrative or spending responsibilities, but constrained decision-making

authority. In dualist federations, constituent units don't have the obligation to administer federally legislated programs, but their powers can be constrained by concurrency and a heavy reliance on conditional transfers.

Some former British colonies that became federations (United States, Canada, Australia) were based on the dualist model, so that federal departments are present throughout the country delivering federal programs. Dualist federations often have areas of concurrent federal and constituent-unit powers—for example, agriculture in Canada— but even so, there can be parallel federal and constituent-unit departments working side-by-side. Against this, the "continental" systems (Germany, Switzerland, Austria, Spain) are more integrated in that the constituent units typically administer federal programs in areas of concurrency. The Latin American federations are basically dualist; that of South Africa is integrated; and Nigeria, India, and Pakistan have elements of both.

Both systems have strengths and weaknesses.

- In principle, the integrated model provides for national policy frameworks, while permitting constituent governments the latitude to adapt these to local circumstances. In practice, however, such federal laws are often highly prescriptive and leave little discretion to constituent units. German federalism addresses this by empowering the Länder governments to vote in the Bundesrat on federal legislation affecting them. Over time, this requirement for majorities in both the popularly elected lower house and in the upper house led to frequent deadlock. After reforms, fewer laws now need the approval of the upper house. Excessive entanglement has also been an issue in Spain, where the central government has negotiated new arrangements with some autonomous communities to limit the central government's use of framework legislation to enter into certain areas of local interest.

- The dualist model tends to produce less entanglement, but it can lead to duplication or even programs working at cross-purposes. And while constituent units are not normally obliged to administer federal laws, federal legislation is almost always paramount in areas of concurrency. Dualist federations are particularly subject to debates over the federal government's using its spending power to influence consitutent-unit programs in areas beyond federal legislative competence.

2.4 Spending power

Most federations permit both orders of government to spend in areas beyond their legislative jurisdiction. Such a spending power can be used by federal governments to significantly increase their role, notably in federations where there is little concurrency of legislative jurisdictions.

In all federations, one order of government cannot make laws in areas of the other order's exclusive jurisdiction. However, many powers are not exclusive, and most federations also have some areas of concurrent jurisdiction where federal law is almost always paramount. As well, integrated federations can have constitutional provisions giving constituent units the sole responsibility to administer federal laws— effectively, to do the spending—in certain areas of concurrent jurisdiction.

Beyond these allocations of legislative and administrative responsibility, most federations have constitutional provisions or court rulings that permit governments to spend on any object, even in areas where they could not legislate. So, for example, a constitution may assign education to the constituent units, but this still does not preclude the federal government from having spending programs in the area of education so long as they do not constitute legislation. Central governments frequently use this spending power to influence the programs and activities of constituent units in areas beyond federal legislative competence. The spending power is most important in federations where there are few concurrent powers and the constituent units have exclusive legislative powers in important areas that the federal government wishes to influence.

Legal Provisions around the Spending Power in Some Federations

The central governments of **Australia**, **India**, and **Malaysia** have explicit constitutional authority to spend in areas beyond their jurisdiction. The central government of **Spain** has such a power, subject to strict limits imposed by the courts. The constitutions of the three oldest federations, the **United States**, **Canada**, and **Switzerland**, did not mention a spending power, but each employs it to some degree. In the United States, the Supreme Court has interpreted the federal power to levy taxes for general welfare to permit the spending power. The Canadian Supreme Court has neither affirmed nor denied federal and provincial spending powers, and, in the past, the federal government made much use of it, though not in a manner constituting legislation in an area of provincial jurisdiction. A recent federal-provincial agreement, however, requires a majority of provinces to approve of new spending initiatives in areas of provincial competence and allows provinces, under certain conditions, to opt out with compensation. While the Swiss constitution does not establish a spending power, in practice the only check on federal spending would be through a referendum, which has not happened. The spending power is much less controversial in integrated federations. **Germany**, for instance, has many concurrent jurisdictions, in which cases federal laws must be approved by a weighted majority of Länder votes and then administered by the Länder. **Belgium** is unique, in that its constitutional court has restricted federal spending to areas of federal legislative competence.

Federal governments may use their spending power in three ways:

- to make **general-purpose transfers** to the constituent-unit governments so as to increase their fiscal capacity to meet their responsibilities;

- to make **conditional program transfers** to the constituent-unit governments, requiring them to implement certain programs in a defined manner;

- to create **directly administered federal programs** in an area normally viewed as an exclusive competence of the constituent units.

Constituent units usually have no problem with the first spending power, and the third is relatively infrequent. Most controversy is around the second power, conditional transfers, which may permit a federal government to have strong influence in an area of exclusive constituent-unit competency. Such influence can affect their priorities, especially if matching contributions are required. As well, in some federations, such spending can have a strongly partisan element by providing more program funds to constituent-unit governments aligned with the central government's ruling party.

Defenders of the spending power argue that it allows a federation to adapt and respond to changing circumstances and national priorities. This can be especially relevant in older federations with constitutions drafted in a pre-modern era. The use of the spending power is usually in areas where there is a federal interest in national standards—for example, health care or education—and is consistent with a view that few major subject areas can be neatly defined as exclusively of federal or constituent-unit interest. In practice, the spending power features in the operation of virtually all federations, and is especially important in federations where the constituent units have important exclusive legislative powers. Often the issue is as much over *how* it is used as *whether*.

- There can be legal (Germany) or politically agreed (Canada) rules requiring some level of constituent-unit consent.

- There can be varying degrees of conditionality so as to give constituent units more or less flexibility to design programs that meet national objectives.

These issues are further developed in Chapter Five.

2.5 *Distribution of expenditure responsibilities*

While there are important commonalities in the allocation of powers to the two orders of government in federations, there are

also significant differences. There is a greater commonality in the distribution of expenditure responsibilities than of revenue-raising responsibilities across federal systems.

The biggest government spending programs are typically defence, health care, transfers to individuals, social assistance of various kinds, education, and infrastructure. The following gives a sense of the broad patterns in the allocation of major legislative powers relating to these in federations:

- **Defence**: This is always federal, though Australia and the United States reserve a restricted role for constituent units to raise militia. While defence spending in most federations is 2 to 4 percent of GDP, it is notably higher in Russia and the United States.

- **Health care**: Constituent units usually administer the main programs in this expensive and growing area (government costs range up to 15 percent of GDP), though the federal government usually plays a major role in shaping health programs, whether through its legislative or spending powers. Federal governments can administer certain programs directly (veterans, pensioners, aboriginals).

- **Unemployment insurance, income security, social welfare, and pensions**: These are either concurrent, joint, or federal responsibilities with rare exceptions (in India, states are responsible for unemployment insurance; in Belgium and Austria, consitutuent units are responsible for social services).

- **Education and research**: Primary and secondary education are almost always administered by the constituent units, though the federal government may have concurrent power with paramountcy. Post-secondary education and research show no clear pattern, but federal governments typically play a significant role (sometimes with exclusive competence for post-secondary institutions; sometimes through financial support, notably in student aid). Federal governments usually lead on research spending.

- **Infrastructure**: Federal governments frequently play a key planning and financing role in major infrastructure, though implementation may be by constituent units. Local infrastructure is usually the responsibility of the constituent units. This is an area where the role of the public sector versus the private sector varies greatly, and, in many cases, the former has diminished with time. While, in principle, federal governments should focus on nationally significant infrastructure, for political reasons they are often drawn into very local infrastructure projects.

Federations differ significantly in the share of direct spending (after transfers) that is done by the central versus the constituent-unit governments. Federal governments account for between 32 percent (Switzerland) and 85 percent (Malaysia) of total government expenditures after intergovernmental transfers. There appears to be a trend to greater decentralization of spending in several federations. Variations in spending patterns across federations are wide, though less than variations in pre-transfer revenue shares.

Patterns of Direct Spending in Various Federations

Switzerland, **Canada**, **Belgium**, and **Germany** are the federations where the federal government spends least—between 30 and 40 percent of total expenditures—after intergovernmental transfers. In Germany, and to a certain extent Switzerland, this reflects the responsibility of constituent units to deliver some important federally legislated programs, while in Belgium and Canada it reflects more devolved legislative as well as spending responsibilities. Federal government spending in most federations (**India**, **United States**, **Russia**, **South Africa**, **Spain**, **Austria**, **Mexico**) falls within a range of 45 to 55 percent. In **Australia**, **Nigeria**, and **Brazil**, federal spending approaches 60 percent, though it falls well short of the highly centralized federations of **Venezuela** (78 percent) and **Malaysia** (84 percent).

2.6 Mandates: Funded and unfunded

Some federations permit the federal government to impose expenditure obligations on constituent-unit governments, without necessarily providing revenues to meet the obligation. There may

also be constitutional obligations on constituent governments to meet certain standards.

There is a significant difference between having the **authority** to spend and having the **obligation** to spend. In integrated federations such as Germany and Spain, the constituent units have an obligation to carry out federal laws and constitutional provisions; at the same time, it is normally expected that they are provided adequate revenue-raising powers or transfers to meet these obligations. However, there can be occasions when the spending obligation is not met by adequate revenue provisions. In the 1990s, the German Länder of Saarland and Bremen successfully sued the federal government on the grounds that they had not been provided adequate funds to meet their constitutional obligation to ensure government services equal to those provided elsewhere in the country. However, in 2006, the Constitutional Court ruled that such grants shall be provided in the future only in case of a "state of federal emergency." Consequently, it will be much more difficult for a single Land to claim such bailout payments in the future. A number of constitutions, such as in Brazil and South Africa, set out various principles or rights to certain basic services that could have major spending implications, but usually these are not judiciable.

The United States federal government has a broad (if uncertain) authority to impose mandates on the states, requiring them to execute a federal policy. There was an annual average of two to three of these mandates in the 1970s and 1980s and states complained that they were often unfunded. A reform in the 1990s has limited their use, but has not prevented the imposition of an extremely costly mandate relating to anti-terrorism. States complain as well about costly conditions attached to federal program aid and often call these "unfunded mandates" as well.

Chapter Three

The Structure of Tax Regimes

3.1 Own-source, shared, and transferred revenues

Federal revenue regimes are characterized by their use of three major elements: own-source revenues for each order of government, shared revenues, and federal transfers. Approaches across federations differ greatly.

The allocation and management of taxing and other revenue powers within federations are intimately linked to the system for sharing taxes and effecting fiscal transfers from the federal government to the constituent units. Some federations rely heavily on shared taxes and transfers to fund constituent units, while others emphasize own-source revenues.

Own-source revenues are those that are raised by each order of government using its constitutional power to impose tax and charge fees within its boundaries. Such revenues can be obtained from either an **exclusive** or **concurrent** constitutional authority. Concurrent authority gives both orders of government the power to impose a tax or charge on a particular source, though the power of constituent units to determine their tax or charge may be constrained.

Many federations have **shared** taxes. These are taxes that are typically federally legislated and collected, and distributed by formula among federal and various constituent-unit governments. When the formula is binding, the revenue is sometimes considered "own-source" because each government has a right to its share of the tax; but we shall restrict "own-source" to taxes and charges under the control of a government.

It appears inappropriate to designate shared taxes as own-source for constituent units. Their governments usually have little or no say in determining the tax or the sharing formula, and their share of the revenues may exceed—even greatly exceed, as in the majority of Nigerian states—what was collected within their borders. The constituent units' portion of shared taxes may or may not appear in the consolidated revenues of the federal budget. Both shared taxes and fiscal transfers can be by formula and without conditions, but even formulaic and unconditional fiscal **transfers** are rarely viewed as own-source. The absence of consistency among experts on these terms means there is a lack of standardized data that makes numerical comparisons across federations difficult.

This chapter focuses on the structure of tax regimes, including various principles that may shape them. Chapter Four looks at the allocation of specific revenue sources, while Chapter Five examines tax sharing and transfers.

3.2 Devolved versus centralized revenue raising

Federal fiscal regimes differ greatly in the extent of constituent-unit autonomy to determine own-source revenues. Autonomous revenue powers can promote political accountability and responsiveness to local preferences, but a significant decentralization of the tax system brings risks for economic efficiency, administrative simplicity, and equity. Transfers from the federal government and the sharing of federally levied taxes are alternatives to decentralized revenue regimes.

In federations, the federal government almost always raises more revenues (including borrowing) than it uses directly. This imbalance reflects the stronger logic for devolving expenditure responsibilities rather than revenue-raising responsibilities. However, practice varies from federations where the constituent units raise most—even almost all—of their own revenues to those where constituent units raise only very small amounts.

Revenue Raising in Various Federations

Federal governments raise the lion's share of revenues in most federations. In **Nigeria**, the federal government raises over 90 percent of all revenues, which reflects its control over oil revenues. Federal revenues are around 90 percent of the total in **Mexico**, **Russia**, and **Malaysia**; between 70 and 85 percent in **Argentina**, **South Africa**, **Australia**, **Belgium**, and **Brazil**; 60 to 65 percent in **Germany**, **Austria**, **Spain**, and **India**; and about 55 percent in the **United States**. Federal revenues are less than half of total government revenues only in **Canada** (47 percent) and **Switzerland** (40 percent).

Perhaps the strongest argument in favour of constituent units' having extensive autonomy to finance their own needs is that it clearly links their spending to the raising of funds. This should make these governments more responsive to their respective populations' desired mix of taxes and spending (bigger versus smaller government). Certainly, there are markedly different mixes of taxes and spending between constituent units in some decentralized federations. For example, in Canada, a standardized measure of "fiscal effort" shows Quebec to have significantly higher taxes and spending per capita than neighbouring Ontario. Some believe that such autonomy also makes constituent units more likely to manage their debt responsibly because they are exposed to its cost and less likely to seek or get federal bailouts. Constituent units may also value some autonomy in tax design, no matter the overall level of taxes. Such design is not policy neutral and constituent-unit governments may have objectives that they wish to pursue through tax policy; e.g., in redistribution or in disfavouring certain types of consumption or activity (such as alcohol or local environmental damage).

Against this, devolved tax regimes carry risks for the healthy functioning of an economy because constituent units can adopt taxation policies that distort locational decisions regarding the use of resources, erode governments' collective ability to tax a particular source, and add significant administrative and compliance costs.

Devolved regimes may also pose equity problems if constituent units' capacity to raise revenues varies because of their relative wealth, though this may be counterbalanced by various transfer and equalization arrangements run by the federal government. One of the most devolved federal revenue regimes is in Switzerland; their experience shows that a highly devolved regime can function even in a small country, though it poses numerous challenges.

3.3 Assigning individual revenue sources

The case for assigning individual revenue sources to federal versus constituent-unit governments differs greatly by source. Economic principles such as efficiency, equity, and administrative simplicity are important. Other factors such as constitutional provisions, history, regional politics, and the priority given self-financing can also shape arrangements. One principle can conflict with another, so there is no best assignment of revenue sources.

If constituent units control certain tax sources, there is a risk that some will compete through lower rates to attract investments, labour, economic activity, or residents to their jurisdictions. Locational decisions based on tax considerations instead of economic fundamentals result in a misallocation of resources and undermine the efficiency of an economy. This problem is most acute with tax bases that are relatively mobile, as when some taxpayers can choose where to locate their activity or residence. While it is a matter of degree, typically, real property and natural resources are effectively immobile; some manufacturing (including the processing of resources) or service businesses, the choice of where to work and live, and the location of some retail business are more mobile, especially over longer periods. In practice, the degree of mobility in a federation will depend on distance, language, and culture, as well as on the location of large historic investments in plants, facilities, and infrastructure. Large corporations, with activity across a federation, can sometimes move certain activities quite easily.

or incomes

Competition for mobile tax bases (at its limit, a "tax war") can undermine a tax base itself. Certain constituent units may keep lowering their rates to attract capital, labour, residents, or activity. Other jurisdictions may lower their rates to remain competitive, thus **hollowing out** the tax base—as happened in Canada and Australia where the constituent units bid the inheritance tax down to zero; a similar "race-to-the-bottom" on this tax seems to be underway in Spain.

Equity considerations arise with different revenue sources because of their distribution across the federation. We shall see this most dramatically where natural resources are important, but some federations have very unequal distributions of large corporations, rich people, or retail activity. Such inequality may be dealt with through various redistributive arrangements such as equalizing transfers or sharing federal taxes.

Some revenue sources can be devolved to constituent units with few or no extra **administrative costs** for governments, businesses, and individuals, while others prove very complicated or expensive to levy or collect on a devolved basis.

While no federation has constituent units that are entirely self-financing, one criterion to be considered in the allocation of tax sources is their size or **adequacy**, given the needs of constituent units. Many of the tax bases most clearly appropriate for constituent-unit governments are relatively small, so the criterion of adequacy can be an important consideration favouring constituent units' access to certain tax bases, even if this may pose efficiency, equity, or cost issues that may require compensation.

Few federal constitutions were written with much attention to the economic criteria for allocating revenue responsibilities. Many important taxes—income and corporate taxes, payroll taxes, value-added taxes—were scarcely dreamed of when the first federal constitutions were written, so the assignment of revenue powers in many constitutions can seem very general, obscure, or outdated. For example, in many federations, sales taxes have been a principal revenue source for constituent units; this type of taxation has been increasingly criticized as inefficient, but its replacement by value-added taxes has proven difficult in some federal contexts. In other federations, the federal role in income tax is secondary or constrained, and this, too, can pose problems. And in many federations, constituent units' access to own-source revenues is severely limited. Such assignments may have evolved through court interpretations and political compromise. Even so, considerations of efficiency, equity, administrative cost, and adequacy are constants as federations examine, debate, and adjust their fiscal arrangements.

3.4 Concurrent tax bases and tax room

In many federal systems, certain individual tax bases are available to both orders of government rather than being assigned to one or the other. This can have a number of advantages, but also raises issues of tax harmonization and the sharing of "tax room."

Several federal constitutions provide concurrent authority for both orders of government to levy taxes, such as income, excise, or sales taxes, on the same source. This is different from sharing federally levied taxes, since constituent units have autonomous powers to set rates and sometimes to define the tax base itself. Concurrent tax jurisdiction has both advantages and problems.

One advantage is that both orders of government can have access to large revenue sources, which helps address the criterion of adequacy. At the same time, when the two orders of government co-occupy a tax source, the federal government can often play a central role in promoting a harmonized approach. In some such cases, the authority of the constituent-unit governments may be limited; for example, in Spain, autonomous communities may determine income-tax rates only within the centrally defined base categories and for the one-third of the income tax that is allocated to them. (Scotland in the United Kingdom and the regions in Italy also have limited powers to make marginal adjustments to certain centrally determined taxes.)

Where both orders of government have full concurrency and are completely free to determine their own taxes on a source, say personal income tax, they face the issue of their respective shares of taxes from that source. The room to extract taxes from any particular base is limited—e.g., if all profits were taxed away, companies would go bankrupt or evade taxes—and so the space occupied by one order of government can constrain the ability of the other to raise taxes from the same source. This issue of **tax room** typically evolves over time.

During World War II, federal governments in Australia, Canada, Switzerland, and the United States increased their share of tax collections dramatically. Canada did this through formal "tax rental" agreements and, after the war, entered new agreements whereby "tax points" were vacated by the federal government and then reoccupied by the provinces. The Australian and Swiss federal governments have never vacated the tax room they occupied (though the Swiss government must get regular renewals), while the United States federal government's share has effectively ceded some tax room over the half century, but with significant fluctations in particular periods. Of course, the amount of tax room available is not fixed, but is a policy judgment.

Finally, there is often more than one way to tax the same item, so that, even when the assignment of revenue-raising responsibility provides different taxing authorities to the two orders of government, both may use these distinct authorities to extract revenues from what is essentially the same source. For example, in federations where the constituent units control natural resource royalties, federal governments have used export taxes, corporate taxes, and excise taxes to get a share of resource rents.

3.5 Tax competition

Devolved tax regimes open the possibility of tax competition, which can have both advantages and costs. Controlling destructive tax competition can be done in various ways.

At one level the idea of different governments in a federal system being able to decide their own taxes is very attractive—it promotes accountability, responsiveness, experimentation and self-reliance. At another level, it conjures up concerns of a tax jungle, heavy administrative and compliance costs, and destructive competition.

Some experts argue that tax competition makes constituent units more responsible because if they overtax mobile tax bases they will see them move away and more accountable because their citizens can compare their taxes with those in other jurisdictions. However, competition can promote beggar-thy-neighbour policies that erode a mobile tax base. It can also lead to locational decisions being made on the basis of taxes, not underlying economic factors, and so impose hidden costs on an economy.

Switzerland illustrates strong tax competition in a small federation: for example, an upper-middle-class taxpayer might pay three times more income tax in one canton than in another, so some have chosen to commute to low-tax cantons rather than reside where they work. Brazil has had a tax war with states competing for foreign investment through breaks on the value-added tax. Tax competition has also been a consistent feature of American federalism.

There are two main ways to address destructive tax competition:

• centralizing revenue decision-making in the federal government, which has been the option of many federations;

• harmonizing key taxes of the different jurisdictions, which is a challenge of decentralized regimes.

As well, equalization arrangements may make poorer constituent units feel less need to compete for mobile taxpayers.

3.6 Tax harmonization

Tax harmonization between jurisdictions can limit destructive tax competition and avoid a tax jungle. Harmonization is easier if the federal government plays a major role in a tax field, or has other levers to influence constituent units.

Tax harmonization is pursued in most federations where different governments share a field of taxation. It can be **vertical** between the federal and constituent-unit governments or **horizontal** between constituent units. Both can be important. It is usually system-wide, but sometimes a federal government reaches asymmetric harmonization agreements with only some constituent units.

Governments can harmonize a tax **base** as well as a tax **rate**. A tax base (say for income tax) is defined in terms of different categories (level of income), with definitions (what constitutes income), permitted deductions (such as costs of earning income, or of children), and so on. The tax rate is the amount of tax applied to the different categories in the base (say zero percent below $15,000; 10 percent for the next $15,000; and so on). The advantages of harmonizing a tax base across jurisdictions lie in simplifying the tax system, reducing administrative and compliance costs, and enabling collection by a single tax authority. It also permits different jurisdictions some flexibility regarding their rates, though the ease of doing this varies by the field of taxation. If there is a risk of destructive competition, both the base and the rates can be harmonized, but this obviously constrains the freedom of constituent units (and perhaps of the federal government, depending on the arrangement).

Tax harmonization is most likely to succeed where the federal government plays a major role in setting and collecting taxes from a tax base. It can then leverage its lead role to create a harmonized system, usually with some consultation and mutual adjustment with the constituent units. As well, federal governments may offer or arrange to collect harmonized taxes, which can save constituent units (and taxpayers) money.

Some federal governments have legal powers that permit them to establish rules for constituent unit taxes. For example, the US Congress, drawing principally on the interstate commerce power, can declare its intent to make the federal government the primary source of law in a field and expressly pre-empt the states from passing laws in the area (even if they do not contradict a specific federal law) or pre-empt state tax laws having certain characteristics. This power has been used to constrain state powers in relation to sales taxes and personal and corporate income taxes.

Tax harmonization between constituent units but without federal government involvement has had few successes. Federal leadership usually depends on the federal government's having a major role in regard to a revenue source. The European Union has no independent taxing power at the centre, but has considerable institutional resources to promote a single market. However, with the EU's virtual absence of central taxes, harmonization has proven very difficult and some member states use their tax systems to encourage the migration of certain taxpayers and activities and even to facilitate tax evasion.

3.7 Tax administration

Tax administration systems should apply tax laws uniformly to achieve an optimum balance of high collection yield and low collection cost. The collection cost should be acceptable to both governments and taxpayers, and the system should promote voluntary compliance. While tax administration systems may be centralized or decentralized, a single centralized system is typically more efficient where a tax base is shared with the federal government.

Tax administration is a complex technical responsibility that requires clear and consistent interpretation of a tax law by those who collect the tax. A healthy tax administration system relies heavily on the quasi-voluntary compliance of taxpayers in filing tax forms, and this is more likely to work well in a country with high literacy, good records, and professional standards of public administration. Such systems should be well-staffed, properly accountable to the governments imposing the taxes, and appropriately transparent.

In federations, tax administration can be centralized or decentralized, even when the decision-making on taxes is not. There are three basic models, which can be combined in different ways:

- Each government collects its own taxes. In almost all federations, at least some taxes are collected by each order of government.

- The federal government collects taxes for the constituent units. Whether by constitutional provision or by delegation, the federal government's administration acts as an agent for the constituent units. This model works especially well in cases of harmonized joint tax fields and may produce both significant administrative savings and higher tax yield.

- The constituent units collect taxes for the federal government. This is unusual, but is the basic model in Germany and Switzerland. It appears this model may be significantly more expensive for both taxpayers and administrations, and poses challenges for consistent application of tax rules.

Tax Administration in Various Federations

In **Australia**, the federal government collects all federal taxes, including the value-added tax whose revenues are reserved for the states. States collect their own taxes. In the **United States** and **India**, both orders of government collect their own taxes. **Canada's** federal tax agency has provincial representatives on its board: by agreement, it collects virtually all federal taxes and the personal, corporate, and value-added taxes for some provinces; Quebec collects all its own taxes as well as the federal value-added tax in Quebec. In **Spain**, each order of government normally administers and collects its own taxes, and the central government collects shared taxes; the exception is in the Basque country and Navarre where, by historic arrangement, these two autonomous communities collect all taxes, from which they pay a levy for their share of the expenses of the central government. In **Malaysia** and **Russia**, the federal government administers and collects taxes for the constituent units. The least common arrangement for tax administration is for constituent units to collect for the federal government. **Germany** is the main example: the Länder participate in decisions on federal taxes through the Bundesrat. In **Switzerland**, the cantonal and local governments collect all taxes.

Whatever the institutional structures for tax administration, there are many technical issues that require resolution, such as double taxation and tax avoidance. There must be rules determining in which constituent unit an individual or corporation is considered to be resident, as well as where profits, losses, or certain transactions are deemed to have happened. Such rules can be part of a harmonized regime, or akin to international arrangements on double taxation. Within federations, one government may not be able to tax another, which can be especially important for lands and corporations owned by governments. This situation can be addressed through special arrangements that are equivalent to taxes; for example, in Canada, the federal government makes payments in lieu of taxes on federal properties (but the provinces make no payments of corporate income tax to the federal government from their publicly owned utilities).

Chapter Four

The Allocation of Specific Tax and Revenue Sources

4.1 Types and value of revenue sources

The size of government revenues relative to the economy varies greatly across federations, reflecting different levels of economic development, resource endowments, and philosophies of taxation and government. A few major revenue sources typically dominate government incomes, but the importance of individual sources differs markedly between federations. Typically, the federal government has access to all major revenue sources, while the constituent units may be limited to less lucrative sources; but there are important exceptions.

The level of government revenues in federations reflects a country's economic development, the philosophy of government and taxation, and, in some cases, natural resource endowments. The revenue shares of all governments in federations range from less than 20 to almost 50 percent of gross domestic product: the highest yields are in certain European federations, which are both rich and supportive of a strong welfare state, while the lowest yields are in certain developing country federations with weak public infrastructure and few natural resources. Seemingly similar countries can have very different levels of government revenues: Austria's 43 percent versus Switzerland's 29 percent; Canada's 34 percent versus the United States' 25 percent; Brazil's 37 percent of GDP versus Mexico's 19 percent.

While societal factors have a broad influence on the size of government in federations, the actual performance of a particular federation can change rapidly. Tax revenues grew dramatically in Australia, Canada, and the United States to meet the needs of World War II. Since 2000, government tax revenues have declined slightly on average in OECD countries, but experience varies from countries that continued to rise to those, such as Australia and Canada, where there have been substantial drops after successive rounds of tax cuts. In some cases, a new tax regime can have a dramatic impact. Argentina, for example, had a long history of low tax yields (less than 15 percent of GDP), but in less than ten years it doubled its yield with economic recovery and the imposition of export and financial movement taxes. Of course, federations that are very dependent on natural resources have seen dramatic swings in total revenues because of highly volatile petroleum and other commodity prices.

Income taxes are very lucrative in all industrialized federations and are often the most important single revenue source; they are much less important in federations with developing economies. Value-added, sales, or turnover taxes are important in all federations. Social insurance contributions, which are typically a payroll tax, vary from being the largest single revenue source in some industrialized federations to non-existent in others; payroll taxes for other purposes tend to be minor. Natural resource revenues can vary from being by far the dominant source to non-existent. Import and export taxes are usually quite minor, though they are significant in a few federations with developing economies. Property taxes are a common feature of taxation systems, but their value is usually a small fraction of more important sources and varies a good deal among federations.

Federal governments typically have significantly greater revenue-raising power than do constituent units: they usually have access to all the most important revenue sources, while constituent units can be significantly more restrained and limited to less lucrative sources. There are, however, cases where the *federal* government has significantly constrained access to a potentially important revenue source: sales tax in India; income tax in Nigeria, Switzerland and the Basque country in Spain; VAT in Brazil; resource revenues in Australia and Canada. This lack of full access may result in the federal government's adopting taxes that are less efficient than those it would have chosen if it was not constrained.

4.2 Personal income taxes

Personal income taxes are generally very important in industrial-ized economies, but much less so in developing countries. The federal government usually has the largest share of them, but many federations permit the constituent-unit and local govern-ments to levy them as well. When constituent-unit governments levy income taxes, there are strong advantages to their operating within the framework of the federal government's tax regime.

Personal income taxes are the largest revenue source, representing 40 to 50 percent of total government revenues in Australia, Canada, Germany, and the United States. The taxes can be quite progressive, with higher rates on higher incomes, and therefore serve as effective instruments of redistribution. Income taxes are usually limited in less developed societies because of lower cash incomes and difficulties with a system based on widespread voluntary reporting (which requires a largely literate population); as well, extensive tax evasion may discredit income taxes as a redistributive tool. South Africa is an exception among developing countries and manages to raise one-third of revenues through a federal income tax.

Where the federal government is seen to have a strong lead role on "equity" within a federation, the redistributive potential of income taxes (which can include refundable tax credits for the poor) is an argument for their centralization. This case is even stronger if taxable income is defined to include more mobile sources of income such as income from capital. The mobility of the income tax base will vary with the geography of the federation (it may be easy to reside in one constituent unit and work in another), language and culture (citizens are often attached to their linguistic or cultural region), and employ-ment opportunities. While the case for a federal lead on the income tax is strong, the potential importance of this revenue source is itself an argument for constituent units having access to it. As well, some constituent units may have their own equity objectives that they would wish to pursue through the income tax.

In practice, constituent units often have a constitutional right, along with the federal government, to levy personal income taxes. In some federations, cities may also be permitted to levy an income tax. When both (or all three) orders of government occupy this field, there are strong economic arguments for harmonizing the base while permitting the constituent units (some) flexibility on the rate structure. However, there have been federations, notably Switzerland, where some constituent units have used aggressively low rates to attract high-income earners as residents, which may have eroded the income-tax base across the country.

Income-Tax Assignment in Various Federations

In the **United States**, the federal government dominates income taxes, but some states also levy them on their own bases (and some states permit municipal income taxes). In **Mexico**, too, the tax is, in principle, concurrent but overwhelmingly federal, though states have a special small-taxpayers tax. In **Brazil**, all three orders have the constitutional right, but in practice the states are allowed a supplementary rate on the federal tax (but inheritance and some capital gains are state taxes). In **Canada**, income tax is concurrent and the provinces, except Quebec, once levied their share through a surcharge; recent reforms give them greater flexibility to tailor rates and rebates, which has made the system more complex. In **Australia**, **Russia**, **South Africa**, and **Belgium** (with a very small, local income tax), the federal government sets and collects income taxes (though they may be shared, as in Russia). In **Germany**, income tax law is federal but requires the consent of the Bundesrat representing the Länder. Income taxes account for 30 percent of total government revenues in **India**, where the central government taxes non-agricultural income and states tax agricultural income. The **Nigerian** federal government has access only to income taxes on its own employees and residents of the capital territory while states have the rest; the tax is underdeveloped. Income taxes in **Switzerland** are collected about equally by communes, cantons, and the federal government, and the system is quite competitive.

4.3 *Corporate income taxes*

Corporate taxes have been a significant source of revenue, but, in many cases, a declining one. There are strong reasons for centralizing these taxes or ensuring they are part of a closely harmonized regime.

Taxes on corporate profits are linked to personal income taxes, in that they are a tax at source on profits that could be distributed to shareholders or capitalized and taxed as income (including capital gains). Thus, governments should design their taxes on personal income, dividends, and corporate profits in relation to one another. Corporate taxes also permit governments to extract a tax on profits that would go to foreign shareholders, but other mechanisms, such as withholding taxes, can achieve the same result. In most countries, corporate taxes have been tending downwards in importance because the international mobility of much corporate investment is forcing governments to be competitive in this regard.

Given the typically strong role of federal governments in personal income taxes and the links between personal and corporate taxes, it is logical that central governments play a key role in corporate taxes. The administrative complexity of dealing with corporations that operate in many parts of the federation further strengthens the case for centralized, or strongly harmonized, design and administration of corporate taxes. Such centralization will reduce the costs of compliance by firms, establish rules about the deemed allocation of profits to various constituent units (if needed), and protect the integrity of internal capital markets. In practice, most federations in the developing world have centralized corporate taxation. While some of the older federations—notably Canada, Switzerland, and the United States—do permit both orders of government access to corporate taxes, this has necessitated measures, of varying success, to harmonize the system.

4.4 *Sales, value-added, and turnover taxes*

Value-added taxes have been widely adopted to replace less efficient sales and turnover taxes. The VAT has proven to be

lucrative and economically efficient, but, unlike sales taxes, is difficult to design and administer on a devolved basis.

Many federations used to have provisions permitting constituent units to levy sales and turnover taxes of various kinds. These conventional sales and turnover taxes were imposed on the total value of a sale or transaction and revenues from them were usually significant. They were quite simple to administer and easy to manage on a devolved basis in federations. As well, sales and turnover taxes are usually not a significant redistributive tax, so central governments concerned with equity did not always see a major need to influence them (though in many developing countries they were the most important source of taxation).

There were a number of problems with conventional sales and turnover taxes:

- If they became too onerous (say 10 percent), they seemed to induce a good deal of tax evasion and even smuggling.

- Taxing goods and services that were inputs to further production added to the cost of final products, especially those with long production chains, and destroyed the level playing field.

- Domestic production suffered relative to imports, whose inputs were not taxed.

- Finally, in a federal system, these taxes could encourage cross-border shopping to evade taxation, or to find lower rates.

In the 1950s, a French tax official invented the value-added tax, which was a new kind of consumption tax designed to address the inefficiency of sales taxes. Since then, the majority of advanced- and middle-income countries (and several less-developed countries) have adopted this form of taxation and, in many cases, it is the largest, or one of the largest, sources of revenue. While a value-added tax has advantages, it poses special challenges in federations when constituent units can set their own bases and rates.

A value-added tax is ultimately a tax on the consumption of a final product or service. However, it is levied at each transaction in the chain of production as businesses buy inputs and sell their outputs onward to other businesses until the final product reaches the consumer. Each business collects the VAT at its point of sale, but is credited for VAT it has already paid on its inputs; thus, on any one transaction, the net new tax is only on the "value added" at that stage in the chain. The final consumer pays the last business the full amount of the VAT. This system ensures a neutral tax regime (unless there are exemptions) that taxes all final products the same, however many steps they may have gone through in production. The final feature of the VAT is that it is normally refunded when a product is exported so it is not a "tax on exports." And the VAT applies to all imports.

It is evident that this system depends on a high level of compliance by businesses all along the chain. When it works well, it permits much higher levels of efficient taxation than conventional sales taxes because it is non-distortionary in not favouring products or services with shorter production chains. The system can also increase other tax payments, such as business and income taxes, because it brings greater transparency to what is happening in the economy.

All major federations, except the United States, have adopted a VAT, at least in part. (In the United States and some other federations, constituent-unit sales-tax regimes are being eroded by mobility and the Internet.) Brazil combines a federal tax on industrial goods with a state VAT on other goods. Brazil and Argentina have maintained significant turnover taxes alongside the VAT because the federal government in Brazil and the provinces in Argentina have limited alternatives for raising own-source revenues that they do not have to share. These turnover taxes are economically less efficient that a VAT because they do not involve credits.

The European Union, which has quasi-federal features, demonstrates the problems of a highly devolved VAT regime. It promoted an EU-wide VAT by defining a common floor of tax rates to escape the distortions created by cascading sales taxes in its internal market. However, there is no central taxing authority, so the EU has gone through several stages and still has only a "transitional" VAT regime. Its central problem is that each member state can vary the base rate and create special provisions and exemptions. With the abolition of fiscal border controls, the European Commission wanted to move to an **origin-based** regime where the VAT rate would depend on the location of the supplier, not a **destination-based** regime that depended on the location of the buyer. However, because rates differed so much, member states would have received very different benefits from these alternatives. As they could not agree, a hybrid regime with many special arrangements was adopted. The EU has also had major fraud problems with the VAT, which arose with the elimination of border controls. The EU's experience contains valuable lessons for federations.

While an origin-based system is easier to administer in that it does not require cross-border sales to be closely monitored, it has the disadvantage of taxing production rather than consumption, which can distort the location of production activities. A destination-based system avoids these distortions, but requires self-assessment by firms buying and selling across internal borders when there are distinct VATs in the constituent units. A federal administration is a virtual necessity as part of such a regime, but, even so, the administrative complexity can be very expensive for governments and taxpayers. A purely federal regime is a great deal simpler and cheaper.

One final complexity with value-added taxes is the sharing of proceeds. This has been a major stumbling block to progress in Europe and Brazil because origin-based and destination-based regimes can have very different results in terms of where the taxes are collected. This matters if constituent units have a claim on their "own-source" revenues, especially if the federation has weak equalization arrangements. Australia, which has a very strong equalization regime, allocates all of the VAT to the states, but does not do so on the basis of either origin or destination; instead, the VAT proceeds are part of the funding of the country's general-transfer regime to the states, including transfers to achieve equalization. Germany is similar.

Some federations don't permit constituent units to levy consumption taxes; however, many do because sales taxes were once viewed as principally local. Where this right to levy sales taxes has been devolved, the successful introduction of a VAT in a federation requires political will and consensus, strong administrative systems, and simplicity of approach. Perhaps the most successful example is Australia, where the states were persuaded to buy into a new, federally run VAT regime, partly because the courts had defined their taxing powers very narrowly; in exchange, the states keep the VAT proceeds. Canada and India have made modest progress, while Brazil has a seriously distorting VAT system that cannot be changed without unanimous consent.

Value-Added Taxes in Various Federations

In **Nigeria**, **Russia**, **Switzerland**, and **South Africa**, only the central government can levy a VAT or special-consumption taxes, and all have some form of VAT. (**Spain's** situation is similar, except in the Basque country.) In **Malaysia**, this tax is also a federal prerogative, and there are plans to replace the current sales and services taxes with a VAT. In **Canada**, the federal government persuaded some provinces to give up their provincial sales taxes in exchange for a VAT that the federal government administers on their behalf; Quebec has accepted the structuring of its taxes along these lines, but administers its own (not fully harmonized) VAT as well as the federal VAT on a delegated basis with a system of credits. **Germany** has a national VAT decided by the federal government and the Länder, and administered by the Länder.

In **Brazil**, the federal government can apply a manufacturing tax on a narrow base of industrialized goods, and must share revenues with state and local governments; the states and local governments can apply a VAT on other goods and are free to set their own rates on a base defined in the constitution. This has led to intense competition to attract investment and greatly eroded their tax base. Moreover, as the VAT is collected at origin, the poorer northern states have done less well, so there are now different rates for northbound and southbound goods, which has resulted in tax evasion.

Argentina introduced a federal VAT as part of major reform in 1974. In the 1990s, it promoted a fiscal pact that prompted the elimination of the provincial turnover sales tax on the manufacturing and primary sectors, and managed to greatly increase returns. With modernized administration, the VAT goes into a pool with certain other taxes that are shared with the provinces. VAT revenues collapsed in Argentina's economic crisis and have only slowly approached their former level, despite the high rate.

Since 2005, **India's** states have progressively agreed to replace the sales tax with a harmonized VAT, but the destination-based regime is weak in terms of compliance and design, with many distorting taxes still not integrated into the VAT, and no tax credits on interstate trade services included.

4.5 Social insurance contributions and payroll taxes

Social insurance contributions, which may be administered as a deduction from payroll, can be a major revenue source and are a broad-based alternative to consumption and income taxes. Other payroll taxes are typically minor and their revenues can be used for general purposes. They can be managed effectively by both orders of federal governments.

Payroll taxes in the broadest sense are taxes deducted at the point of employment and they can include income taxes, social insurance contributions, and non-income-related taxes on employment. Income taxes are usually considered separately. However, social insurance contributions are often considered a payroll tax when deducted at source, and they are used in many federations to fund social insurance, health insurance, unemployment insurance, workers' compensation, and pension schemes. In some federations, such as Germany, these taxes are essentially a charge on employment, unrelated to income, and serve as a general-purpose tax. In a few federations, such as Belgium and Austria, payroll taxes for social insurance are the largest revenue source and are almost always administered by the federal government. Payroll taxes for social security are very high in Brazil and have encouraged a black-labour economy; however, the major growth in earmarked contributions for social security programs has come from turnover taxes. Most other federations make limited use of payroll taxes.

While payroll taxes are typically heavily federal—Australia is an exception—they are, in principle, good candidates for devolution to constituent units because they are relatively simple to administer. Where constituent units use them to fund social insurance programs, issues such as the portability of benefits between constituent units need to be addressed.

4.6 Property taxes

Property taxes are very suitable to be a local or constituent-unit tax and are typically decentralized in federations, often being the most important source of tax revenues for local governments. The importance and design of property taxes vary widely.

Property taxes are the classic local tax for a number of reasons. The tax base is immobile, benefits are often tied to the tax, the yield is quite stable, and the taxes are effectively administered at the local level. While in most federations these taxes are predominately local, in some, such as Russia, the constituent units have a role as well. In Brazil, urban local governments control taxes on their property, while it is a federal responsibility in rural areas. In Argentina, all three orders of government collect property taxes: the federal government on personal assets, including property; the provinces on rural property; the municipalities on urban property. Administratively, constituent-unit governments (and in South Africa, the central government) may specify the tax base (normally in terms of the value of properties), while local governments then set their own rates.

Property taxes are the primary source of local finance in federations such as Australia, Canada, and the United States, but are much less significant, in absolute or relative terms, in continental European federations, where local governments typically have much larger responsibilities. Because municipalities in some federations rely so heavily on the property tax, there is some speculation that property (especially business property) is overtaxed, but the evidence is unclear. Some US states have experimented with alternate sources of local revenue, such as sales or personal income taxes that piggyback on state administration and collection. Some developing countries have had real difficulties effectively implementing a property tax because of weak capacity and expertise at the local level.

Because local governments may have very different abilities to raise revenues from property, their constituent-unit government may have some arrangements for equalization among local governments.

4.7 Natural resource revenues

Natural resource revenues vary from negligible to dominant in federations, and can be collected in many ways. Where they are significant, a key issue is the control and sharing of these revenues between the central government, and the producing and non-producing constituent units. These revenues can be either highly centralized or very decentralized.

Natural resource revenues are very different from those from other sources because they can be so variable among federations as well as among constituent units within federations. In federations, the most important natural resources are oil and natural gas, which can produce huge government revenues, but coal, metallic minerals, and diamonds (South Africa) are significant in some federations. Timber and water (especially when developed as hydroelectric power) can also produce significant revenues, especially at the constituent-unit level. What all these resources have in common is that their extraction or development costs may be a small fraction of their market value, so that what is known as a **resource rent**, which is the extra margin of value beyond normal returns, is available for the resource owner or governments to extract and distribute in some way.

In such federations as Nigeria, Russia, and Venezuela, natural resource (especially petroleum) revenues dominate or are the largest source of public receipts; they are also very important in Australia, Brazil, Canada, Malaysia, and Mexico. (They are critical in the emerging federations of Iraq and Sudan, but neither has truly resolved how they will be managed and shared.) Even in federations, such as Argentina, India, and the United States, where they are not of major significance nationally, natural resource revenues can be very important for some constituent units. Against this, there are the resource-poor federations in Europe where natural resource revenues are of no significance.

Resource-rich countries face special challenges of economic and political management. A booming petroleum industry can cause the currency to rise and undermine the competitiveness of other industries (the so-called **Dutch disease**). The large potential rents for government can be an invitation to **corruption**. These are the "curse of oil" and potentially the curse of other valuable resources too. As well, because resources are almost always concentrated in only some parts of the country, there are frequently tensions around the roles of the central and regional governments over who controls the pace of development, local environmental protection, and the sharing and spending of revenues. High and volatile prices and the issue of climate change add to this brew.

Because natural resources are immobile, there are few technical difficulties with their being controlled and predominantly taxed at the local level. However, local control can give rise to conflicts if resource-rich jurisdictions are aggressive in driving the pace of development or in offering incentives that make other sectors elsewhere in the country less competitive. The greatest difficulties with local control and taxation arise around sharing when resources are very large and regionally concentrated. In principle, inequities can be remedied by equalization transfers, but this may be difficult if the federal government has limited access to natural resource revenues and there is no sharing between constituent units. While there are strong arguments for a significant federal role in relation to natural resources that have a major importance in an economy, there are also important local interests—in terms of economic and environmental impact—that need to be accommodated.

Whatever the principles, the practice in federations varies considerably. The federations with very old constitutions—Australia, Canada, and the United States—give control of natural resources and revenues predominantly to the constituent units (though the United States government controls extensive petroleum-rich "federal lands" within some states). The more modern constitutions typically give the exclusive or greater role to the federal government, though in Russia this was achieved only recently. Where the federal government does control onshore resources (India, federal lands in the US), there may be some sharing arrangements with the constituent units where production takes place and even with local municipalities (Brazil). In Argentina, the provinces' natural resource ownership was constitutionally reinforced in 1994, though the federal government still has significant management levers and access to revenues.

Offshore resources are almost always federally owned because they lie outside the boundaries of constituent units. Arrangements vary: often there is no sharing of offshore revenues (United States, India), but a few federations (Australia, Nigeria) have made some sharing arrangements with the contiguous constituent units and even with local governments as well (Brazil). While the federal government in Canada has retained formal ownership, it has ceded all these federal resource revenues to the contiguous provinces.

The owner of the resource has the right to royalties, but may impose licence fees, production sharing, local content regulations, and equity arrangements (e.g., through state oil companies). While "ownership" of natural resources is important, other constitutional powers and levers matter as well. For example, in India, the states own onshore minerals, but the federal government extracts the larger revenues and has management control. Federal export controls, price controls, and taxes can be critically important in determining the value of a commodity within the country.

Governments can strongly influence the pace of development and also determine the manner in which they extract rents:

• Some petroleum-exporting countries have imposed restraints or taxes on exports to create protected, below-market prices for local consumers, to slow development, to raise revenues, or to protect energy security. In Malaysia, Pakistan, and India, governments have fixed prices to consumers and been caught having to cover large subsidies (over $20 billion in Venezuela when oil was well over $100).

• Alternatively, the federal governments in the United States and Canada controlled or taxed petroleum imports for many years to promote the development of their domestic industries.

- Corporate, local, and environmental taxes can also affect the pace of development and revenue shares (though typically governments have not used them aggressively).

- Local land-use and environmental controls have been used to stop development, e.g., by some US states in relation to the federally controlled offshore.

Many developing countries make extensive use of government-owned oil companies, and they may receive significant (or even all) of the government's petroleum revenues as payments from these companies. (For example, Pemex's payments to the Mexican government have reached around $100 billion annually.) These companies may not operate on a normal commercial basis or be subject to tax. Arrangements in such cases can lack transparency.

When resource revenues are very large, there can be questions about trying to stabilize their impact on budgets and perhaps about longer-term saving:

- **Stabilization funds** or procedures may be established to deal with the swings in petroleum revenues. Government spending in a particular year can be based on average prices over a preceding period or some nominal price, rather than actual revenues, with any surplus being saved and any deficit being drawn from savings.

- **Longer-term savings funds** may be set up to provide future generations with income once the resource is depleted.

- As well, holding resource revenues as **offshore savings** can limit their impact on inflation, the exchange rate, and the competitiveness of other sectors of the economy.

Stabilization and longer-term savings funds are more typically found at the federal level, but Alaska and Alberta are examples of constituent units that have versions of them.

Onshore Oil-and-Gas Revenue Arrangements in Various Federations

In **Russia**, the world's largest oil-and-gas producer, most of the producing regions' governments get a 5-percent share of oil revenues and none of gas revenues. The federal government has established two petroleum-revenue funds for stabilization and longer-term saving respectively. In **Nigeria**, where petroleum revenues typically represent over 80 percent of all revenues, producing states get 13 percent of government oil revenues from their state on top of whatever revenues they would receive otherwise; the federal government retains revenue above a moving average-price target in a stabilization account, but some states are contesting this arrangement. **Venezuela** also normally depends on petroleum for over 50 percent of public revenues; these are controlled by the federal government in a highly centralized regime, but a share is reserved for the states. **Mexico** channels surplus oil revenues initially towards any emergency or disaster relief deficits, and then into a federal stabilization fund (40 percent), a state oil company fund (25 percent), a states' revenue stabilization fund (25 percent), and a states' infrastructure fund (10 percent) up to a ceiling: beyond that, surplus revenues are allocated equally to four other funds (for federal, state, and oil-company infrastructure investment, and the national pension scheme). In **India**, the union government controls major oil projects, but provides a share of revenues to the producing state, as is the case in **Malaysia**. **Brazil's** central government shares both onshore and offshore resources with the producing states and local municipalities (some of which have benefited greatly).

Hydro power is a renewable resource that produces high-quality electricity. It has frequently been developed by federally or constituent-unit owned or regulated corporations, with a policy objective of providing cheap electricity for consumers and industry rather than swelling government revenues. Thus, the policy may be to charge only what is needed to cover the costs of capital and operations, not to realize the full value from the market (especially when export prices might be high). In Quebec, for example, it has been estimated that the province could generate an additional \$5 billion in revenues by moving to market prices. Such diversion of revenues from governments to consumers is usually not captured in fiscal arrangements that make transfers to constituent units based on their fiscal capacity, though a case could be made for doing so.

4.8 Licences and user charges

There has been a shift to "user pay" as part of the new public administration. User fees have been adopted by all orders of government, especially those providing local services. Such fees are usually modest revenue producers, often yielding less than the full cost of the service.

User fees and licences can be important revenue sources for local or constituent-unit services that are private in nature, such as water, telecommunication and electricity utilities, garbage, and recreational facilities—in South Africa, for example, they account for 40 percent of municipal revenues. Tolls on roads and bridges can be significant. These fees are also called **benefit taxes** since they pay for a specific benefit provided. User fees can recover costs and promote efficiency, though they might be burdensome for poorer residents. They are also easy to administer since it is a simple fee-for-service principle. Historically, many municipalities and local governments did not recover the full costs of such services, but in recent years a number of federations have encouraged this.

Charging for public services is not appropriate when it results in problems of access to a public service that is considered a right or an important long-term investment. Health care and education have both been viewed this way in many federations. That said, user fees are sometimes imposed to avoid overuse of a service that is relatively discretionary or of longer-term economic benefit to the user. As well, in developing countries, user fees can be imposed as a revenue-raising measure even on basic services such as health and primary education.

4.9 Other revenue sources

Various other revenue sources can be important for governments in federal systems: import levies; export levies, especially where

there are large resource exports; excise taxes; environmental levies, which could become increasingly significant because of climate change; payments from publicly owned corporations; and receipts from the sale of assets.

Historically, import levies were important in many federations, but there has been a move to lower or eliminate them because they undermine the efficiency of the economy by encouraging production that is not to a country's comparative advantage. Export levies result in domestic prices that are lower than open-market prices for a good, which creates distortions through an inefficient subsidy for consumers and lower prices for producers of the product. Russia's largest source of oil-and-gas revenues is an export tax. As a result of its economic crisis, Argentina's federal government greatly devalued the peso in 2001 and introduced large export taxes, which fell heavily on the big producers of agricultural and energy commodities in certain provinces. The export tax was meant to be transitional, but has become part of the established structure of Argentina, in part because such revenues are attractive to the federal government in that they are not legally shared with the provinces. The extent of the export tax on agricultural produce has been a major political issue, pitting producers and consumers, as well as different provinces, against one another.

Excise taxes are specific to particular products or services, such as alcohol, tobacco, gasoline, luxury goods, entertainment, hotel rooms, parking, and gambling. As these examples show, they are usually targeted at a particular type of consumption that is deemed unhealthy, anti-social, or insensitive to price. Environmental taxes are also a type of excise tax, in this case targeted at a specific environmental pollutant. Excise taxes can be criticized if they are seen to create unjustified distortions in consumption or activity. If the taxes are too high, they can also promote cross-border shopping and tax evasion, or, in the case of environmental taxes, the "export of pollution" to less demanding jurisdictions. Given the policy purposes of such taxes, they can be appropriately levied by both orders of government. But, in some cases (climate change), these may better be federal, while, in others (gambling), the constituent units, or even local governments (hotels, entertainment, parking) are more suitable. Some federations are also discussing cap-and-trade regimes for greenhouse-gas emissions;

companies may have to pay for emission permits, which could in due course become a significant source of government revenue.

Finally, sales of assets (corporations, land, etc.) and of some public goods (broadcasting spectrum) can result in significant revenues, as can payments to governments from corporations they own: these may or may not be included in the calculation of rights and obligations for fiscal sharing and transfers. An important federal dimension to public corporations is whether one order of government can tax a corporation owned by the other order. Where this is not possible, there can be an incentive for a government to maintain ownership of the corporation because it would lose the value of the tax benefit should the asset be sold.

Chapter Five

Intergovernmental Revenue Sharing and Transfers

5.1 The roles of revenue sharing and transfers

Federal governments raise more revenues from taxes and borrowing than they need for their own direct spending. Federal governments always share some taxes or make fiscal transfers to help constituent-unit governments meet their revenue needs, to effect redistribution within the country, or to promote federal government program objectives. The importance and manner of such revenue sharing and transfers differs greatly among federations.

The logic of centralizing revenue collection is generally stronger than that of centralizing expenditure responsibilities. While the extent of devolution of revenue collection (including borrowing) and expenditure varies greatly among federations, in all cases the federal government assumes part of the responsibility for financing constituent-unit (and even local) government responsibilities. This can be done either by sharing certain (or all) federally collected taxes or by making transfers from the federal government's own budget.

Revenue sharing and transfers serve various purposes. They can contribute to the **general financial requirements** of all constituent-unit (and local) governments, and can be used to **reduce disparities** in the fiscal means of these governments. Federal governments can also make conditional transfers that promote their **policy objectives** with the other tiers of government. Health care, social services, and education are among the largest drivers of government spending in modern welfare states, and these responsibilities are usually heavily borne by constituent-unit governments with some federal assistance.

Tax sharing and transfers combined account for over 90 percent of constituent-unit finances in Nigeria, Mexico, and South Africa; for just under half in Austria, Germany, India, and Australia; and for 13 to 25 percent in Canada, Switzerland, and the United States. Constituent units that have a larger degree of self-financing are typically more autonomous.

5.2 Legal provisions governing revenue sharing and transfers

Constitutions and laws can be permissive or directive regarding revenue sharing and transfers.

The legal basis for revenue sharing and fiscal transfers is found in constitutions, federal laws, and intergovernmental agreements. A legal instrument may be mandatory or simply enabling. Constitutions can set out certain broad principles, such as uniform living standards (Germany), reasonably comparable public services at reasonably comparable levels of taxation (Canada), or equitable sharing of revenues (South Africa). They can also set up commissions to recommend the details of such sharing (India, Nigeria, Pakistan, South Africa), but this can also be done outside the constitution (Australia). In three cases (Germany, Ethiopia and South Africa), the constituent units have a formal role through the upper house in deciding the sharing of revenues.

The relative costs and priorities of major programs change over time so there is a need for periodic adjustment in revenue sharing and transfer agreements. For this reason, the precise details of such arrangements are rarely found in constitutions, though the courts may play a significant role in interpreting constitutional provisions (Nigeria, Germany). In many cases, the arrangements are determined in federal laws.

5.3 Tax sharing versus fiscal transfers

Federations differ in their approaches to tax sharing versus transfers. The approach chosen can have implications for the criteria of financial support, for the autonomy of constituent units, for certain economies of scale, and for fiscal stabilization.

Tax sharing and fiscal transfers are the two principal means by which constituent units receive revenues from federal governments. **Tax sharing** usually designates a part of a federal tax or taxes for allocation to the constituent units; in some cases, these sums do not appear in the federal budget because they are treated as constituent-unit revenues. **Fiscal transfers** are made from the federal government's general revenues and do appear in the federal budget as an expense.

There is a great variety of approaches to both tax sharing and fiscal transfers, but the following are some ways in which they compare:

- **General-purpose versus program-specific purposes**: Tax sharing almost always provides general revenues to constituent units, as opposed to financing for a particular purpose. Fiscal transfers are also frequently for general purposes (in which case they are unconditional), but they can also be made for particular programs (and subject to very specific or quite general conditions).

- **Formula versus discretionary**: Tax sharing is usually done by an established formula, which may be in place for a number of years (five in India and Nigeria). Such sharing formulas can be legally entrenched so that the federal government cannot change them during the designated period. When this is so, the revenue share is transparent and predictable, though its absolute level may fluctuate widely. Transfers, too, can be based on long-term formula arrangements, but they are also frequently short-term and more discretionary. Even when nominally long-term, they may be subject to change within the designated period if the federal government so decides (as happened in Canada in the 1990s when the federal government dramatically cut transfers as well as its own spending).

- **Capped versus uncapped**: Tax-sharing arrangements are less likely to include revenue caps than are fiscal transfer arrangements. Thus, as revenues from a shared source rise, the share going to the constituent units usually rises directly with it. Fiscal transfers, by contrast, are more likely to involve specified amounts or amounts tied to some measure of need or expense, but with a ceiling on the size of the transfer.

These points describe tendencies in the form and use of tax sharing versus fiscal transfers, but with ingenuity both approaches can be— and have been—designed in almost any way imaginable, so that, for example, there can be tax sharing that is conditional, discretionary, and capped. As well, the boundaries between the two can blur: in the United States, the federal excise tax on gasoline is reserved for sharing with the states for the interstate highway system, but this is done through conditional transfers not direct tax sharing; Canada's federal government now does something similar in indirectly providing gasoline excise-tax revenues to municipalities through the provincial governments.

Constituent units can have a high level of dependence on shared taxes or transfers. Some experts believe this is not a problem so long as the rules are clear and subject to "hard" constraints that induce constituent units to behave responsibly by not running large deficits and expecting to be bailed out by the federal government. Other experts argue that, whatever the rules, a very high degree of constituent-unit dependency on federally sourced revenues effectively creates a liability for the federal government to bail them out in extreme circumstances, and can encourage irresponsible policies on the part of constituent units.

In regimes where tax sharing is important but only some federal taxes are shared, the federal government can have an incentive to raise those taxes it does not have to share, and this can affect the structure of the tax regime. Such **gaming** of taxes happened in Brazil. In India, the Union Government had engaged in tax gaming, but it has since put all federal taxes into the pool for sharing to avoid this problem. Gaming may also be a factor in the Argentine federal government's imposing heavy export taxes on agricultural and energy commodities; these taxes are not shared with the provinces. As well, Argentina's sharing scheme has different sharing arrangements for different taxes, so there are winners and losers according to which taxes are changed.

The mix of support flowing to constituent units from tax sharing versus transfers varies greatly, but inconsistencies in data collection make it impossible to give precise numbers.

5.4 Tax-sharing criteria

When large pools or sources of taxes are shared, there are usually multiple criteria for sharing, including some measure of need. The principle of derivation holds that some or all of the revenues raised in a jurisdiction should stay there and provide a net benefit. Federations balance the principles of derivation and equity in different ways.

When taxes are shared, there must be decisions made on the respective vertical shares to the two (or sometimes three) orders of governments, as well as the horizontal shares among the constituent units (and perhaps local governments). The formulas for such sharing can be quite simple (e.g., a percentage share going to the constituent units, based on population), but very often they are complex and bring in several factors, such as where the taxes were collected (derivation), population, territory, equality of constituent units, and other measures of fiscal capacity or of need.

The concept of derivation relates to a broader set of issues of "fiscal flows" into and out of each constituent unit. Calculating such flows can present major difficulties. Should import taxes collected at a port, or corporate taxes collected from a headquarters, or an excise tax collected at a distillery, or even a personal income tax collected where an individual resides (but does not work) be attributed to the jurisdiction where they are collected, even though what is being taxed may come from or be destined for other jurisdictions? In countries that use the derivation principle, technical answers to such questions must be found. (Similar issues exist on the spending side of fiscal flows: Should federal spending on a military base or a highway be seen as benefiting only the jurisdiction where it occurred? Which constituent unit benefits from a major purchase, the one where it was produced or the one where it will be used?)

Tax Sharing in Various Federations

The **German** and **Austrian** systems are based overwhelmingly on tax sharing, with Länder having very limited own-source revenues over which they have discretion. **Nigeria** is similar, with the special dimension of a huge reliance on oil revenues collected in only a few states. **Canada**, **Switzerland**, and the **United States** are at the opposite extreme, with constituent units essentially controlling their tax revenues and with negligible or no sharing (but some fiscal transfers). In **Belgium** and **Spain**, constituent units get 35 to 45 percent of their tax revenues from tax sharing; their other revenues are own-source and federal transfers. **Australian** states share all of the federally levied value-added tax, but also receive other significant fiscal transfers. Both **Brazil** and **Argentina** rely heavily on tax sharing with significant revenues going into the sharing pool; however, the federal governments have favoured the development of certain non-shareable taxes (notably export and import taxes in Argentina, and corporate and turnover taxes in Brazil), which has increased their fiscal latitude and centralization. Where taxes are shared, the criteria for apportionment among the constituent units vary greatly. In **Nigeria**, most federally levied taxes are shared with the states according to a formula that includes equality of states, population, area, and fiscal capacity; for the huge oil revenues there is also a special allocation of 13 percent to the producing states. **Pakistan** shares most federally levied taxes on the basis of population, despite major differences in wealth. **India** currently shares all federal taxes based on a formula that includes population, per capita GDP, area, tax effort, and fiscal discipline. Fiscal transfers supplement tax sharing in all these cases.

Tax-sharing arrangements frequently result in significant inequalities between constituent units. When a significant portion of shared taxes are allocated to all states equally, regardless of population, this can create a demand for the creation of new, small states (as has happened in Nigeria). Inequalities in tax sharing can sometimes be addressed by complementary arrangements for equalization transfers and for program specific transfers.

5.5 Sharing natural resource revenues

Natural resource revenues, which are very important in some federations, can be shared or not, in differing degrees, depending on considerations of ownership, derivation, and equity. They can also be treated in various ways in equalization arrangements.

Natural resources tend to be located very unevenly among the constituent units of federations. As well, their cost of development can be very low relative to their value in the market. Thus, natural resources can be a major source of governmental revenues in federations, but these can be distributed in very different ways.

The sharing of natural resource revenues is a source of tension in many federations. There are two opposing principles: **equity** and **derivation**. Equity calls for broad sharing, derivation for a special (or even exclusive) part to go to the producing region. The principle of derivation may be tied to constituent-unit ownership of resources (as in Canada), but it can apply even where the federal government owns the resource (as in Nigeria). Resource-rich federations can have very significant fiscal disparities among constituent units, depending on the sharing arrangements.

There are two distinct issues. First, which governments get what direct access to resource revenues? Secondly, are there equalization arrangements, and, if so, how do they deal with resource revenues?

Either constituent-unit or federal governments can own resources, and ownership does not necessarily confer control or the greatest access to revenues. In Canada, Australia, and the United States, constituent units get the major revenues from resources they own, whereas in Argentina, India, and Malaysia the federal government usually gets the larger share of revenues from resources owned by the constituent units. When federal governments own the resources, they may provide a share of resource revenues to the constituent units where the resource is produced (as in Brazil, Nigeria, Russia, and for federal lands in the United States). As well, some federations provide all (Canada) or a significant share (Brazil and Nigeria) of revenues from federally owned offshore petroleum resources to constituent units (and in Brazil's case, municipalities) that are contiguous with the producing zones.

(In a number of federations, natural resources have been managed with objectives such as low prices for consumers, industrial development, and import substitution, as well as revenue generation. Such approaches, particularly subsidized prices for consumers, can be extremely expensive and result in governments foregoing major revenues. This is true not only of oil and gas, but also of hydro-electricity.)

The allocation of resource revenues can clearly create major fiscal disparities among constituent units in federations. Some federations (Mexico, Venezuela) address this by essentially giving no share of resource revenues to the constituent units where they are produced. Russia gives a small, capped share. Nigeria gives an uncapped 13 percent of federal petroleum revenues to the producing states, so they have much greater fiscal capacity than non-producing states. In Canada, the combination of provincial ownership of onshore resources and the federal transfer of offshore-resource revenues to provinces means that the major resource producing provinces have a significant fiscal advantage with this class of revenues.

Canada has made the unusual decision to treat resource revenues differently from other revenues for purposes of equalization. The argument for doing so stresses the significance of constituent-unit ownership, the non-renewable nature of these revenues (which makes them somewhat comparable to realizing a capital asset as opposed to ordinary income), and the possible disincentives to resource development if these revenues are treated like others. The argument against doing so stresses "a dollar is a dollar," and that ability to spend (or actually spending) is more important than the source of revenue, the risk of economic distortions from discounting such revenues, and the lack of evidence of disincentives to development. Canada's equalization program now gives non-renewable natural resource revenues a 50 percent weighting in calculating equalization entitlements, which means that resource-rich equalization-receiving provinces end up with a higher fiscal capacity than resource-poor equalization-receiving provinces. Australia's program treats resource revenues like other revenues.

5.6 Conditional versus unconditional transfers

Federations vary in the extent, number, and types of fiscal transfers. Fiscal transfers are particularly important in federations that do not have extensive tax sharing, but some federations mix both about equally. Transfers may have no conditions, or minor or major ones. Conditional transfers, especially those requiring matching funds, can skew the priorities of constituent-unit governments.

Fiscal transfers are the alternative to tax devolution and tax sharing as a means to increase constituent-unit fiscal capacity. In some federations, such as Canada, Mexico, Switzerland, and the United States, transfers from the federal budget are the main form of fiscal support from the central government to the constituent units (in each of these cases except Mexico, the constituent units have significant own-source revenues). Other federations, such as Australia, Belgium, Brazil, India, and Spain, make roughly equal use of tax sharing and fiscal transfers. Still other federations, such as Austria, Germany, and Nigeria, heavily favour tax or revenue sharing, though in Germany's case fiscal transfers are also important.

Fiscal transfers can have different characteristics:

- They can be **legal entitlements** or **discretionary**. In the former case, constituent units can appeal to the courts to enforce them, while in the latter the federal government has the power to decide. Typically, large grants are legal entitlements, while smaller program grants can be more discretionary. In many federations, intergovernmental agreements cannot legally bind the federal government.

- They can be **conditional** or **unconditional**. Conditional grants must be spent for a particular purpose, though the degree of conditionality can vary considerably from highly detailed to very general. Unconditional grants are for general spending purposes and they include equalization transfers. "Block" transfers fall somewhere between conditional and unconditional grants, in that they may be linked to a specific program area (such as health), but have only very general principles or terms associated with how the money is spent and minimal reporting requirements.

- Conditional grants can be **cost-shared** or **contributory**. Cost-shared grants require the receiving constituent units to match federal financial support for a program in a prescribed manner. Contributory grants occasionally cover all of the costs of a constituent-unit program that the federal government wishes to see implemented, but more usually they are a contribution to the general costs of programming in a specific area. Large "block grants" for major areas such as health or education can take this form.

Conditional grants can encourage constituent units to spend more on programs that are priorities for the federal government. In some cases, the federal government gives such grants because the constituent units may under-spend in program areas (such as education, research, and major infrastructure) where only part of the benefit of a program may be experienced locally while other benefits spill over across the country. In other cases, it may want to encourage common equity standards, or more coherent program designs that facilitate individual or corporate mobility across constituent units. Or a federal government may simply wish to support a particular program, activity, or investment that its legislators or executive favour for ideological or voting-seeking reasons.

Federal governments cannot ensure that all of the funds they provide for a particular purpose go to increase what the constituent units would have spent anyway, and the empirical evidence suggests that typically there is some leakage. As for unconditional grants, evidence indicates that they result in a higher overall level of constituent-unit program spending than would happen if the equivalent money were transferred directly to residents, with the constituent units then having to tax it back. Good grant design provides incentives for constituent units not to drive up program costs (so federal grants are tied not to actual spending but instead to some established norm for costs) and to spend efficiently (so grants are tied not to inputs but to outputs); there may also be caps on the grants. Conditional grants have been more common in dualist federations, where federal governments do not have the legal power to establish framework policies within which constituent units must operate.

Conditional Grants in Various Federations

The **United States**, driven by its congressional system, imposes at least some conditions on all transfers to the states; it has 600 categorical and typically very detailed grant programs and 17 block grants. In addition, each year Congress approves several thousand "earmarked" projects (such as a bridge), which individual legislators append to laws as a condition of their support; these may be cost-shared with states. While the **Swiss** constitution does not permit federal conditional grants, in practice certain grants are made for particular programs, though largely with the consent of the cantons (which could challenge such conditions through a referendum). The largest grants in **Canada** are now block transfers targeted to "established programs" such as health care and social assistance, with minimal conditions. While **Indian** states' main support from the federal government comes through unconditional shares of federal taxes, they also receive fiscal transfers, and less than half of these are conditional grants for development plans and various centrally determined projects. In **South Africa**, the constitution requires transfers of an equitable share of federal revenue to provinces, to which the federal government can and does attach conditions for its expenditure. **Australia** has large unconditional transfers to the states, but also some 100 conditional programs, which are to be transformed into a handful of less conditional transfers. Most grants are conditional in **Austria**, **Switzerland**, and **Germany**, while rarely so in **Brazil**, **South Africa**, **Russia**, and **Belgium**. Conditional versus unconditional grants are roughly balanced in **Mexico**, **Australia**, **India**, and **Malaysia**.

5.7 Horizontal fiscal inequalities

The wealth and fiscal capacity of constituent units in federations varies considerably, especially in developing countries. The issue

**of sharing wealth within a federation is closely tied to citizens'
sense of solidarity with the federal and regional communities.
There are also economic arguments for (and against) redistribution to poorer regions. Sharing can be done in various ways.**

All federations have disparities in the average wealth of the populations
of their constituent units. These disparities range from quite small to
very large: for example, the ratio of the poorest constituent unit's gross
domestic product per capita to that of the richest unit is about one
to 1.4 in Australia, one to two in Austria, Canada, and the US, one to
three in Germany, one to seven in Brazil, one to nine in Argentina and
in India. Such major disparities bear directly on the revenue-raising
capacity of constituent units, and the prospects for balanced economic
development and equitable availability of public services. The result is
tensions between better-off and less well-off regions.

The principles of derivation and equity conflict in terms of how much
sharing there should be in a federation. In practice, there is a large
cultural element in how the populations of federations view their
"sharing communities": countries such as Australia and Germany put
a high premium on trying to equalize standards, while others, such as
the United States, Brazil, Nigeria, and India, accept much greater
regional differences and put more emphasis on self-reliance. Clearly,
federations with very large disparities between constituent units face a
greater challenge in promoting equalization than do those with lesser
disparities.

The arguments for some measure of equalization are both philosophical and economic. The philosophical arguments have to do with the
culture of sharing or solidarity in a federation, which in turn reflects
the sense of community at the different levels, as well as attitudes to
self-reliance and claims on local resources. The economic arguments
are based on the inefficient allocation of labour and reduced productivity in the national economy that can result from some privileged
constituent units having a more attractive combination of taxes and
services. This **net fiscal benefit** may induce citizens to migrate for
purely fiscal reasons. The argument that equalization provides net
benefits for the whole economy runs up against the counter-argument
that there may be net costs for the richer regions that are paying for

the program. Thus, in richer federations that have very strong equalization programs, the commitment to equalization seems to result more from a sense of national solidarity than from arguments about economic efficiency. (Arguments about sharing exist as well within unitary countries and within constituent units. However, central governments in unitary countries typically tax consistently and deliver much the same level of services across the country, though differences can exist at the level of municipal or regional governments.)

5.8 Equalization programs

Most federations promote some measure of horizontal redistribution to reduce disparities among their constituent units. Some have "equalization" policies, programs, or systems that take an integrated view of government finances and bring constituent-unit governments up to a defined fiscal standard. Others have no integrated approach, though some transfers and tax sharing may include redistributive criteria. Such standards can include revenue capacity or some overall measure of fiscal need. Designing such programs involves significant practical challenges and choices.

Federal systems can redistribute wealth among constituent units in three ways:

- The federal government's direct spending on its own programs can be significantly redistributive in that its revenues come disproportionately from the richer (or more resource-rich) parts of the country, while many of its spending programs tend to be fairly equal throughout the country or even targeted at poorer regions with greater needs.

- Tax sharing and major fiscal transfers can also be equalizing by giving weight to population, need, or other measures that favour redistribution, (though these criteria may also include further criteria, such as derivation, that are not equalizing).

- Finally, there can be equalization programs as such. Federations that promote equalization do not try to equalize the average *income* of populations across the country; rather, they focus on raising the

fiscal capacity of poorer constituent-unit governments up to a specified standard, which may include need and costs. Equalization
programs or policies address inequalities between constituent-unit
governments, not populations.

Some federations have no equalization objectives as such. Mexico has
various sharing and transfer arrangements but no coherent equalization. (However, it, like Argentina, requires that the federal budget
show the geographic incidence of spending.) Nigeria allocates its
revenues on the basis of a number of criteria, the net result of which is
major disparities between states. Similarly, Brazil shares federal
personal and corporate income taxes (while the VAT levied by the states
belongs to them), but the system results in large inequalities between
states. While Belgium has substantial net transfers to the poorer
communities and regions, the allocation of the shared portion of
personal income tax is based on derivation, not equalization. As well,
many federations base their main transfers on a number of criteria,
some of which relate to equalization while others do not. India weighs
population, per capita income, area, infrastructure needs, and tax
effort. Spain's formula is based on population, area, personal income,
fiscal effort, and other factors (and is highly controversial because it
results in inversions, with some poorer autonomous communities
ending up with greater resources per capita than richer ones). Transfers
based on population are effectively equalizing, given that they are
financed out of general revenues, but factors such as area and a
minimum per constituent unit are often not equalizing.

Sometimes, particular programs may have a special equalizing component, in that poorer constituent units receive a large proportion of
federal matching funds for earmarked programs. This is the case in the
United States for Medicaid and states' education grants, and was the
case in Switzerland for some programs. In both countries, the poorer
jurisdictions spent less than richer ones on the matching programs, so
the overall equalizing effect was minor. This was part of the reason
Switzerland overhauled its transfer regime.

Equalization programs can be designed to address disparities in
revenue capacity, or a combination of revenue capacity and expenditure need:

- Each constituent unit's total **revenue capacity** can be estimated on the basis of a representative level of effort for each source. In developing countries with weaker tax administration and data, it is necessary to use proxies such as gross domestic product or income per capita, adjusted if necessary to take into account particularly lucrative revenue sources (such as oil or gas).

- Each constituent unit's **expenditure needs** can also be estimated on the basis of a representative expenditure system, analogous to a representative tax system. Alternatively, proxies for program expenditure needs can be used—from very broad measures such as population and income, to more refined breakdowns that include school-age and aging populations, poverty, and physical terrain.

Both alternatives involve technical challenges and subjective judgments, but these seem greater in assessing expenditure need. A particular issue with assessing need is whether differential costs are included (for example, because of difficult terrain or dispersed population): some economists argue against doing so in a way that would neutralize underlying differences in real costs. Equalization programs should not interfere with incentives for constituent units to spend and tax responsibly. Typically, this means basing the program on **representative** (average or appropriate) taxes and expenditures, not on actual performance, because the latter could result in constituent units gaming the system to achieve an advantage. Whether an equalization program targets revenue capacity alone, or includes expenditure needs, a decision is required on the standard to which the poorer units will be raised or on the formula for sharing a determined pool of equalization funds. These standards or formulas themselves can be complex.

Equalization programs can be of two types:

- **Gross equalization programs** bring poorer constituent units up to some nationally defined standard. Most systems (Austria, Canada, Germany, Russia, and Switzerland) are of this type.

- **Net equalization programs** bring all constituent units up or down to a common national standard. Australia's system is effectively net and takes an integrated view of the entire envelope of central and state revenues and needs. Germany's system was fully net before reunification, but the cost of bringing in the poorer Eastern Länder put a major strain on the system.

Most equalization programs, such as those in Austria, Canada, Germany, and Switzerland, make special transfers to even up fiscal capacity of the poorer constituent units once other revenue sources and transfers are taken into account. Thus equalization programs as such can be relatively small when compared with other transfers or revenue sharing, which can also be equalizing. In Australia, by contrast, the equalization dimension is integrated into the much broader system of transfers to all states. While equalization programs are frequently funded entirely by the federal government, in Germany significant equalization transfers are also made between Länder, and in Switzerland the federal transfers are supplemented by transfers from richer to poorer cantons. Such transfers between units can also enhance transparency about who pays for and receives equalization.

Equalization programs can have perverse effects, though, normally, good design can address them:

- Equalization entitlements can be highly volatile and unpredictable. This situation can be addressed by basing entitlements on longer-term averages and having caps and floors on how much they can vary from year to year.

- Entitlement formulas can provide disincentives for constituent units to raise taxes (for example, if doing so would have little or no impact on their net revenues) or to control costs (for example, if equalization considers actual expenditures). These issues can be addressed respectively through careful design of the formula and the use of normalized revenues and costs.

The United States is an interesting case of a rich federation that does not have an equalization program. Some programs, such as Medicaid, provide extra assistance to poorer states, though their impact does not seem significantly redistributive because poorer states have lower uptake. (As well, some federal programs, such as education assistance, require **intra-state** equalization, mainly to ensure that poor populations and visible minorities receive a fair share.) In terms of broad fiscal flows, federal revenue raising and spending by state does not seem coherently redistributive and seems rather to reflect the strategic positioning of senators and representatives in Congress. Defenders of the American system argue that it has been effective in bringing adjustments in the real economy, as people and jobs migrate. Certainly, the relative wealth of the 50 states has changed greatly over time.

Equalization Transfer Programs in Various Federations

Australia's program addresses both revenue capacity and expenditure need using a large, separately determined pool of revenues to fully equalize all states to a national-average standard. **Canada's** program considers revenue capacity alone (though it discounts natural resource income by 50 percent). It aims to bring poorer provinces up to a national-average standard, subject to constraints on the growth of equalization payments and the overall fiscal capacity of equalization-receiving provinces with significant natural resource revenues. **Germany** has a four-step process: tax sharing; special VAT sharing with the poorest Länder; fiscal transfers from richer to poorer Länder; and, a final federal adjustment, grants/payments, for the poorest Länder. **Austria** has a per-capita federal grant to the Länder to bring average per-capita tax revenue to the national average. **Switzerland** brings poorer cantons up to 85 percent of a national average calculated on capacity and need through payments by both the federal government (two-thirds) and the richer cantons (one-third); smaller, related grants include a federal component that addresses higher costs of urban, mountainous, or poor cantons, and a transitional fund financed by the federal and richer cantonal governments. **Russia** allocates 6 percent of the federal budget to equalization grants for about 60 to 65 regions (of 83) that are below a national-average measure, including capacity and costs. The grants take into account population, revenue capacity, and also the relative cost of the provision of public goods, which varies several times across the regions; the grant raises the poorest regions to a minimum standard.

5.9 *Transfers to local governments*

Municipal and local governments are most often a responsibility of constituent-unit governments, but they can be a constitutionally established third order of government. In either case, they usually have a weak tax base, requiring significant transfers from the other orders of government. Direct political relations between the federal and local governments can create a complex trilateral dynamic.

In most federations, local government is a responsibility of the constituent units, which largely decide the roles of local government, their access to own-source and shared taxes, and any grants they might receive. However, in a few federations—Brazil, India, Nigeria, South Africa, and Switzerland—the municipal level of government is established in the national constitution as a third tier of government, with various defined rights and responsibilities.

Whatever their constitutional status, municipal or local governments tend to have a weak revenue base relative to their responsibilities, and therefore they depend on significant transfers. (Switzerland is an important exception in that its communes raise about a third of all taxes and rely on transfers from cantons and the federal government for less than a sixth of their funding.) Such transfers may come from either order of government, but typically they come predominantly from the constituent units when local governments are their constitutional responsibility. Nigeria provides for federal revenue sharing with the municipal governments, but these funds must pass through the state governments, which sometimes do not make the onward transfer as they should.

Chapter Six

Economic Management in Federations

6.1 Fiscal federalism and macroeconomic management

Central governments in federations typically lead in managing the economy, but constituent governments can have an important influence and role. Both federal and unitary systems of government can have structural vulnerabilities that encourage irresponsible fiscal and economic management. While these vulnerabilities differ, neither type of system has a clear advantage, and both have performed either well or poorly.

Across federal systems, central governments are always responsible for monetary policy (except in the European Union federations that have transferred it to the European central bank). They are usually responsible for raising most public revenues and for determining key features of the tax system, import tariffs, and investment policy. They often lead on strategic investments in infrastructure as well as research. Thus, central governments inevitably lead on economic management, though constituent units have an important secondary role in some decentralized federations.

Many experts have argued that the decentralized nature of federations makes them prone to uncoordinated and irresponsible macroeconomic management. However, the empirical evidence for this assertion is weak or even contradictory. Indeed, the world's most (and least) successful economies include both federal and unitary countries. Some argue that federations are vulnerable to three major weaknesses.

• First, the central and constituent-unit governments may pursue contradictory fiscal and economic policies. There can certainly be cases where the federal government may be pushing the fiscal accelerator while constituent units are applying the brakes, or vice versa, but it is not a general problem in federations and we shall see how some have avoided it. Unitary countries can also have incoherent fiscal and economic policies, sometimes because of differences among the executive, the central bank, and the legislature.

- A second possible federal weakness is that constituent-unit governments have a structural incentive to bargain or manoeuvre for more than their fair share of resources, thus driving up public spending. Again, such a situation can occur, but its extent seems quite limited because central governments can exert control in various ways. There is also ample evidence of "log-rolling" and other practices in some unitary regimes that drive up public spending.

- The third possible federal weakness is that constituent units often incur debt irresponsibly because they count on the federal government to bail them out. Certainly this has happened in some federations, but unitary countries can get into trouble with debt as well. As we shall see below, there are ways for federations to manage this risk.

It appears that other factors are far more important in determining the quality of fiscal management in a country than the choice of a federal or unitary system. The key point is not which system is better or worse, but recognizing that each can have weaknesses and strengths, and that these depend very much on local culture and the particular arrangements adopted.

6.2 Central banks and monetary policy

Monetary policy is centralized in all federations, though the independence of central banks varies from virtually total to minimal. While the fiscal situation of constituent units can be dramatically affected by monetary policy, their governments are essentially excluded from its formulation. Constituent units in turn can impact monetary policy by fiscal decisions, including their use of borrowing.

While monetary policy is normally a federal responsibility, it is conducted very differently among federations (and many have changed their approach dramatically over time). Some have given their central banks complete, or virtually complete, independence to conduct monetary policy, while others maintain political control through the finance ministry. Typically, independent central banks have more credibility than federal finance ministries in maintaining their monetary policies when dealing with political pressures.

Monetary policies can target inflation rates, exchange rates, or other factors related to the performance of the economy. The choice of monetary policy can be important for constituent units in that it affects their cost of borrowing as well as the performance of the economy, which in turn drives revenues and program expenditures. It can also have significantly different impacts on regions within a federation, depending on their main industries (e.g., commodities versus manufacturing).

Brazilian and Argentine experience shows how dramatically monetary policy can affect fiscal relations in federations. After chronic inflation, Brazil committed to monetary stabilization in the 1990s, initially through sustaining the exchange rate of the currency. A wave of financial crises in emerging economies in the late 1990s forced Brazil to move to a floating exchange rate, so that monetary stability became dependent on an inflation-rate target, which, in turn, was backed up by high interest rates and strict management of public spending. This put enormous pressure on state budgets at a time when federal taxes were rising dramatically. The result was a major reversal of the fiscal decentralization that was part of the structure of the 1988 constitution. Argentina also went through a dramatic crisis, in its case in 2001 when it was forced into a huge devaluation of the peso. The federal government turned to an extensive use of export taxes to compensate for some impacts of the devaluation, but these taxes had highly differential impacts among provinces, and greatly increased the federal revenues that did not need to be shared with the provinces.

Of course, constituent units can, in turn, have an important impact on monetary policy. They can adopt fiscal policies that are in conflict with monetary policy (as can the central government when it does not control monetary policy) by being expansionary or contractionary when monetary policy is the opposite. In Canada in the late 1980s, Ontario and some other provinces spent aggressively because of buoyant revenues at a time when the central bank was trying to cool inflation; the central bank responded by being even more restrictive. Some federations have had debt crises brought on by excessive borrowing by constituent units—on occasion, by circumventing borrowing rules and taking on large debts from banks they owned— that then required bailouts by the central authorities.

The European Union's evolving monetary union, bolstered by a common currency in 1999, meant that participating member states could no longer deal, as some had, with excessive accumulations of government debt through inflation and devaluation. Instead, they would need to adjust their spending and revenues within negotiated maximum deficit and debt limits. This is a difficult task with ongoing problems. The same logic applies in all federations that seek to limit the budget excesses of constituent units. In Germany, for example, the federalism reform in 2009 passed a new debt rule linking the Länder to the European Stability and Growth Pact.

6.3 Fiscal policy coordination and stabilization

Fiscal policy typically tries to smooth the cycles of the economy by adding to or subtracting from net demand through government borrowing or surpluses. Federal governments usually play the major role in this regard, especially where constituent units have constrained fiscal flexibility. Good fiscal management can be promoted through common technical frameworks and regular policy dialogue.

Governments manage fiscal policy by spending less or more than their income, thus running surpluses or deficits respectively, and thereby affecting the level of demand in the economy. Typically federal governments have more latitude than constituent units to vary their fiscal policy, particularly to take on debt in periods of economic downturn. Some programs, such as unemployment insurance and social assistance, are natural and "automatic" economic stabilizers with expenditures rising in recessions and falling in periods of growth; it makes sense for the federal government (perhaps with the constituent units in decentralized federations) to play a major role in such programs.

While automatic stabilizers can be important, both orders of government in federations can use their discretion to implement active fiscal policies as well. Approaches to coordinating such policies vary considerably. At one level, developing common budget frameworks and promoting technical dialogue can be helpful in bringing transparency in budgets at the federal and constituent-unit levels, without necessarily constraining the budgetary decisions of governments. Common technical definitions can include major macroeconomic variables— prices, wages, key monetary measures—as well as common revenue and expenditure classifications and fiscal years for all governments. In addition, proper audit and control procedures provide credibility. It can also be helpful if all governments make their budget forecasts well before the beginning of a new fiscal year, and, if there is a forum for discussion and the possible coordination of budget plans, perhaps over a two- or three-year horizon. Predictability in tax shares and federal transfers can be important in helping constituent units avoid unforeseen surpluses or deficits. Finally, contingency reserves against surprises can help with fiscal stabilization. Some of these technical requirements can be imposed within a federal system or negotiated with the constituent units.

Informational and Procedural Measures Promoting Fiscal Coordination in Various Federations

A **German** federal law governing budget management establishes budgetary classification and accounting systems, as well as a multi-year planning framework. **Belgian** federal, regional, and community governments work within an interministerial system that fosters accountability, and all governments exchange data on a monthly basis. **Australian** states report some data into a uniform presentation framework, but may use their own standards for their budgets. **Canadian** provinces take part in regular dialogue with the federal government and accept the standards of the Public Sector Accounting Board, an independent body. **American** states usually adopt Generally

Accepted Accounting Principles (GAAP), but have little dialogue with the federal government on fiscal matters. **Mexico** has had an uncoordinated regime, with major data inconsistencies making it difficult to consolidate a national fiscal account, but has moved to create an integrated accounting regime. **Argentina** also has had a weak system but has made some improvements under its Fiscal Responsibility Law. **Nigeria** has major problems with lack of transparency in national and, in particular, state accounts.

6.4 Debt management and fiscal responsibility laws

Some federations rely heavily on market disciplines, transparent processes, and information, as well as occasional suasion, to manage debt. Others provide formal disciplines on constituent-unit (and sometimes federal) debts, including fiscal responsibility laws or other measures to promote fiscal responsibility. These have had varying success.

Federal governments can be good or bad fiscal and economic managers, but when they do poorly they usually must redress the situation largely on their own. By contrast, when constituent units are poor fiscal managers, and especially when they accumulate excessive debt, the federal government may need to intervene because of the risks that such large debts may have for economic stability and the federal government's own finances.

All federal governments are subject to the twin disciplines of capital markets and their voters in relation to their borrowing and debt. Some federations rely on the same disciplines to manage the debts of constituent units, and the credibility of such a market-based approach depends not only on well-functioning capital markets but also on a widespread belief that the central government will not engage in bailouts. Such credibility may also be enhanced by legislated requirements on balanced budgets or debt control, such as are common with American states and Swiss cantons. In Australia, the central government chairs a loan council that oversees federal and state borrowing, but its role has been largely informational, rather than controlling, and it was redundant in a period of surpluses; the council now also advises on whether total government spending on major capital is consistent with the government's inflation target.

In some federations, voters and market mechanisms are ineffective in disciplining constituent units. As well, when constituent-unit governments rely overwhelmingly on federal-tax sharing and fiscal transfers, the markets may assume the federal government provides an implicit bailout guarantee for constituent-unit debts. In these two cases, the central government may try to control or reach understandings on constituent-unit debt. These measures can include limits on total debt or debt servicing in relation to revenues, permitting debt only to finance capital expenses, requiring federal approval of borrowing, or requiring that borrowing be done through the federal government.

The European Monetary Union is unusual in being a monetary union where the central government's fiscal weight is extremely small (its revenues are just over 1 percent of GDP). Thus, all countries in the monetary union have agreed to three main fiscal targets, with limits on annual deficits and total indebtedness in relation to GDP. Austria, Belgium, Germany, Italy, and Spain have all had to work out arrangements between their central governments and constituent units on how they will meet these targets on a whole-of-government basis. In some cases, they have had only qualified success because of weak constraints on constituent-unit deficits.

Federations in the developing world present a mixed picture of systems with long-established federal controls on borrowing and newer systems that have moved to stricter regimes following credit crises with their constituent units. In some cases, federal controls have gone beyond controls on borrowing to more comprehensive **fiscal responsibility laws**.

Borrowing Controls and Fiscal Responsibility Laws in Various Federations

In 2000, **Brazil** adopted a fiscal responsibility law that was negotiated with the states following the renegotiation of their debts and a prohibition on their issuing new bonds. The law constrains both orders of government, with limits on spending for government employees, on debt (not exceeding a ratio of current revenues), on recurrent expenditures (which must have a matching revenue source), and on short-term spending in election years. It also provides a multi-year planning process and various transparency and oversight provisions (e.g., on contingent liabilities). Tax breaks and new expenditures must be justified with a longer-term impact assessment. Importantly, the federal government can withhold payments to states that do not comply, and criminal proceedings can be brought against elected officials. Since Brazil adopted the law, public sector deficits have fallen substantially.

Following the 2001-02 debt crisis, the **Argentine** government offered to bail out the provinces in exchange for their accepting the Fiscal Responsibility Law to which 22 of the 24 provinces have agreed. The law establishes guidelines to promote consistent and transparent public accounts, limits on expenditures and debt, and sanctions on non-compliant provinces. It also provides for the establishment of fiscal stabilization funds (six provinces have done so in a modest way), which could be important given Argentina's large commodity exports. In 2006, **Mexico** adopted a law on the federal budget and fiscal responsibility that includes provisions for planning, debt limits, transparency of public finances, control of civil-service costs as well as mechanisms for handling petroleum revenues. **Nigeria** passed a fiscal-responsibility and procurement act in 2007, but its application was limited to the federal government alone because the Senate rejected its application to the states; since then, a few states have agreed to join the system.

Indian states can borrow only domestically and require the agreement of the Union government for new debt if they have outstanding loans with it; even so, state debts have risen significantly, partly through off-book devices such as debts taken on by state-owned utilities. The central government has a fiscal responsibility act that obliges the government to show how it will achieve budget balance within a five-year period; however, it excludes the very expensive subsidies for fuel and fertilizer, which are off-budget and do not apply to the states. The **Russian** federal government now strictly limits regional debt and deficits. In **South Africa**, national legislation circumscribes provincial borrowing. The **Belgian** federal government makes agreements with constituent-unit governments on borrowing, based on recommendations of the Higher Finance Council and the national bank.

6.5 Microeconomic policy

Microeconomic policy, which focuses on the efficiency and productivity of the economy, necessarily involves all orders of government in federations. Some federations have strong measures to promote internal markets, and to frame consistent competition and sectoral and regional policies. Others have a diffuse assignment of regulatory responsibility for internal markets and major challenges of coordination. Regulatory policies dealing with natural monopolies, labour markets, capital markets, and environmental standards are particularly important.

An important part of economic management in federations is addressing the operation of the internal market so as to limit barriers to trade in goods and services, to investment, and to the mobility of labour. Open markets within a federation are generally thought to promote the efficient use of resources. That said, the governments of constituent units can often try to promote local interests by favouring them through regulations, tax measures, subsidies, and in other ways. As well, they may sometimes introduce measures for other reasons, such as environmental protection, the provision of electricity, or the improvement of a service, where the way it is carried out creates a barrier within the federation's internal market. The risk of internal barriers tends to be greater where the constituent units have important taxing powers or legislative powers touching economic subjects. Constituent units often own or regulate public utilities, which they can protect as local monopolies closed to competition from elsewhere in the federation.

The challenge of limiting internal barriers is constant in federations because new ones can be created at any time. There are three broad approaches to doing so, which can be combined in different ways:

- **Constitutional provisions**: Federal constitutions can include principles relating to the internal market that permit the barriers to be challenged in the courts.

- **Federal government jurisdiction**: Federal constitutions can empower the federal government to pass laws that constrain or override constituent-unit laws. This is most obvious in cases of concurrent jurisdiction, where federal laws are almost always paramount. A federal power to regulate internal trade and commerce can also be important. Other federal powers, including a power to pre-empt (as in the United States) can be used to limit internal barriers.

- **Collaborative efforts**: Federal governments may not have the legal authority to limit barriers created by constituent units, or they may have the authority but not be prepared to pay the political price of intervening unilaterally to strike down a measure that is popular in a region. In such cases, federal and constituent-unit governments may work together to address internal barriers—and this can be done variously through negotiations, studies, and joint industry-government task forces.

Federations differ in the priority they give to reducing internal barriers and in the approaches they adopt. The European Union, which was founded with the objective of creating a unified market, offers valuable lessons that could be used by federations, including the powerful role of the European Court and the adoption of weighted majority voting, rather than unanimity, to make new rules. While some federations, such as the United States, have relatively strong federal trade and commerce powers, others, such as Canada, do not. Even where the federal powers are quite strong, there are always some barriers that cannot be addressed by federal fiat or by a legal appeal to the constitution, so co-operative mechanisms can be important.

6.6 *Regional development*

Federations may use regional-development policies to address regional economic disparities as a complement to federal transfers and tax sharing. Some federations favour addressing such disparities through economic and social policies rather than through fiscal sharing and transfer arrangements.

Chapter Five presented an overview of tax sharing and fiscal-transfer arrangements in federations, including equalization. Regional development, or other economic development programs, can be used to supplement or substitute for such fiscal sharing arrangements. Many federations have special programs aimed at the economic growth of less-developed regions. In India, for example, the revenue-sharing arrangements proposed every five years by the Finance Commission are complemented by strategic investments proposed by the Planning Commission to promote national and regional development; these can take the form of significant conditional transfers to the states. As well, broad-based federal programs directed at individuals—such as social assistance, unemployment insurance, labour-market training, and pensions—can be an important part of a federation's approach to regional disparities. The European Union, which has very small fiscal resources compared to federal governments, has created funds for investments in poorer member states (less than 90 percent average EU income) and in targeted poor regions, rather than any kind of fiscal equalization program. Such regional development programs seem to be most successful when they upgrade basic infrastructure and the quality of the labour force rather than providing targeted assistance to particular industries.

Chapter Seven

Institutional Arrangements and Issues

7.1 Fiscal forums and advisory commissions

Parliamentary regimes tend to have greater control of fiscal management by the executive branches of governments than do presidential-congressional regimes, where legislatures have more latitude. The structure of the political party system is also of critical importance. Upper houses sometimes play a role in representing the fiscal interests of constituent-unit governments or populations.

Politicians can stay in office only by winning elections, so competitive democratic politics are central to the dynamic of federations, including fiscal management. Politics in every federation are complex and can change quickly on the basis of an election, or series of elections, so that the same major political institutions can function very differently depending on who is in power in which governments. Given this, generalizations about the impact of institutional arrangements on economic and fiscal policy must be approached cautiously.

The major political institutions shape relations and the dynamic of fiscal management in a federation. Most federal governments have either a parliamentary or a presidential-congressional system, and their constituent units usually have the same system. (Exceptions are Russia, which has a presidential-parliamentary system, and Switzerland and South Africa, whose five-member executive and president respectively are elected by the central legislatures, but not subject to votes of confidence.) In parliamentary regimes, the government usually requires the confidence or support of a majority in the lower house to continue in office, while, in presidential regimes, the executive is independent of the legislature. Budgets in parliamentary regimes are a matter of confidence, so there are usually strict limits on the extent to which they can be amended (at least without the consent of the government), while in presidential-congressional regimes the legislature can revise the budget without causing the government to fall.

Presidential-congressional systems are thus often seen as having less-disciplined budget processes, since the executive may need to negotiate extensively with the legislature to win its consent (and the legislature must avoid a presidential veto in some cases). This can be seen, for example, in the extensive insertion into legislation of earmarked projects by the United States Congress, as well as in major revisions to the budgets proposed by the president, especially when his party does not control both houses. Nigeria and Mexico have also been characterized by major changes in budgets proposed by the executive. However, some presidential regimes, such as Brazil and Argentina, have seen budgets proposed by the president approved with few amendments, and this reflects inducements the president can use to keep legislative supporters in line. As well, Brazil and Argentina engage in greater intergovernmental dialogue on fiscal issues than do Nigeria and Mexico.

In parliamentary systems, budget deal-making largely occurs before the budget is proposed and it is driven by the executive. Even if this involves serious compromises (which it can, especially when there are coalition governments, as in India), the deal-making is led by the finance minister and cabinet, not by a legislative committee. It can involve extensive consultations with the constituent units.

These differences affect how fiscal federalism is carried out in different regimes. Where the executive is in control, as in most parliamentary and some presidential regimes, the governments of the constituent units will focus their efforts on influencing the federal government, while in presidential-congressional regimes with more diffuse budgetary power, they often try to influence both the central executive and legislators.

Virtually all federations have upper houses, which are elected or named on a different basis from the lower house (which is usually popularly elected more-or-less on the basis of population). In many cases, representation in the upper house is equal for all constituent units, but even when it is not, the upper house typically over-represents smaller units, so that upper houses have a bias in favour of their interests. However, the powers of upper houses vary greatly, typically being strong in presidential-congressional systems and relatively weak, especially on budgetary matters, in parliamentary regimes. Germany is an important exception, where the Bundesrat, which represents the Länder governments, must approve any law (including any budgetary matter) affecting them; this requirement produced a very integrated system that has sometimes had difficulty making decisions. Ethiopia is a parliamentary federation whose House of Federations is elected by state legislatures (not governments) and has no normal role in legislation, except that it must review and approve budgets as they affect the states; in practice, it has forced budget revisions, despite the dominant party regime across the federation. In South Africa, all bills affecting provincial competencies must be approved by a majority of the nine provinces represented in the National Council of the Provinces, subject to the National Assembly's being able to override with a two-thirds majority.

A number of federations do regular reviews of their federal fiscal regimes and they name commissions to consult and prepare reports on these. India's periodic Finance and Planning commissions, which are named by the Union Government, have been largely successful in that their members are seen as eminent and independent, and their recommendations carry great weight. Against that, Pakistan's experience has been more problematic in that its finance commissioners are delegates under instruction from governments and they must agree unanimously; as a consequence, there has often been stalemate. Australia has for half a century depended on the Commonwealth Grants Commission to regularly review and make recommendations on their fiscal transfers. The commission's board includes members named by the federal government after extensive consultation with the states; there is a large permanent staff. Its recommendations carry great weight and are usually adopted virtually intact.

Canada faced a major fiscal crisis in the late thirties and appointed a royal commission to review federal fiscal arrangements. Its report had a major impact, not just on federal-provincial fiscal relations but on the realignment of constitutional responsibilities, e.g., with the federal government taking on unemployment insurance. More recently, the federal government and the provincial governments both named panels to review certain aspects of the fiscal transfer regime; in the end, the federal revisions were heavily based on the recommendations of the federally named panel.

Federal systems often have well-developed intergovernmental relations, working within sectors and operating at various levels from heads of government and ministers to senior civil servants to technical working groups. In the financial area, it is common to have working groups engaged on financial statistics and accounts, and on tax administration, as well as on major policy matters that will be negotiated among ministers. The strength and depth of such arrangements can depend on the level of development in the country, but also on how institutions function at the highest levels. Thus, the United States has relatively underdeveloped networks for intergovernmental meetings, and states promote their interests bilaterally or through lobbyists; parliamentary regimes, such as Australia, Canada, India, and Switzerland (not to mention Germany with its Bundesrat and especially the different "Minister Conferences" in which the ministers of the Länder meet regularly) are characterized by dense and active networks.

7.2 Courts and dispute resolution

While not all fiscal arrangements between governments in federations are judiciable, many are. Courts can play an important role ruling on fiscal issues related to powers, laws, and the underlying principles of a constitution. Some federations have special courts for tax matters. Some avoid taking certain fiscal matters to the courts, preferring to address them politically.

Courts have played a big role in shaping the constitutional framework of most federations and in ruling on points of importance for fiscal federalism. At the same time, many of the most important issues in fiscal federalism are political, not legal. For example, arrangements around fiscal transfers or revenue sharing are subject to periodic review and amendment, and, typically, the courts play a minor role in such matters, which must be resolved politically. As well, some intergovernmental agreements may deliberately be drafted as political, not legal, documents, which gives them a greater flexibility in administration. Even when there are legal rights and obligations, governments may choose to manage disputes politically or through alternative dispute resolution. South Africa's 1996 constitution emphasizes co-operative governance and limits the access of governments to the courts so that it is a last resort, to be used only after other alternatives have been exhausted. In both Switzerland and Ethiopia, the courts do not have the final say on the constitution: in the former case, it is the population, by referendum; in the latter, it is the House of the Federation, elected by the state legislatures.

Some Court Decisions of Importance for Fiscal Federalism

The **United States** Supreme Court has given interpretations to the interstate commerce power, to the spending power, and to the power of pre-emption that have greatly strengthened federal dominance of fiscal federalism. The **Australian** Supreme Court narrowly interpreted state power to tax, most importantly in four cases in the 1940s that effectively transferred income-tax powers from the states to the Commonwealth government. In recent years, the Court's severe limitation of state tax powers was a key factor in the states agreeing to the new centrally administered value-added tax regime. **Germany's** Constitutional Court found in 1992 that the federal government was responsible for a large share of the heavy debts of several Länder, on the grounds of the constitution's "equality" provisions. **Canada's** Supreme Court found that a federal-provincial fiscal transfer agreement could be changed unilaterally by the federal Parliament, whose sovereignty could not be constrained without a constitutional amendment. **South Africa's** Constitutional Court has so far refused to adjudicate intergovernmental disputes, instead urging the governments to exhaust all mediating avenues before litigating against each other. **Nigeria's** Supreme Court has played an active role in adjudicating disputes over oil between the federal and state governments. In

---

a recent decision, they denied state rights over certain offshore oil deposits. After the ruling, however, the federal government made a deal to split the revenues with the states that had sued and lost.

7.3 Asymmetric arrangements

Constituent units in federations normally have the same formal constitutional powers in relation to fiscal matters, but there are a few exceptions. Asymmetric arrangements are more common through administrative or political arrangements.

Constituent units within federations have very different characters, capacities and needs. Some of them create strong political pressures for devolution, while others do not; some face unique financial circumstances. One way to address such differences is to adopt arrangements that treat constituent units differently. However, constitutional asymmetry can create difficulties if it appears that one constituent unit is receiving greater powers or favourable treatment. The experience in Spain is that special arrangements agreed to with the autonomous communities of the "historic nationalities" are usually sought by the others. At present, the Basque country and Navarre have special fiscal arrangements that permit them to collect all taxes, provide less support for the central government, and use their corporate tax to attract investments; while these arrangements are rooted in history, the asymmetry is creating pressures that are still not resolved. Russia had severely asymmetric arrangements in the early stages of its new federal constitution, but these have been quite systematically eliminated. Against this, the small Borneo states in Malaysia have special constitutional powers over forests, fisheries, and petroleum that relate to their character and method of entering the federation, and these have not led to generalized demands for the same treatment.

Certain kinds of asymmetry may simply be practical, non-constitutional arrangements, where different constituent units work out various arrangements to suit them. Thus, in Canada, the federal government has reached bilateral agreements on tax administration with the provinces, with the offer being similar but the take-up different. In this and in some other arrangements, such as pensions, there is a limited degree of "specialness" to the treatment accorded Quebec, which is largely accepted by the other provinces. Furthermore, there may be no problem in providing special grants to poorer constituent units so long as it is done in a principled, programmatic manner so that all of them get similar treatment. Political problems can arise when the federal government resorts to favouritism for particular constituent units for partisan or other reasons, and this certainly happens in some federations.

7.4 Capitals, territories, and aboriginal peoples

Federations can have special fiscal arrangements for their capitals, territories, and tribal areas or aboriginal lands.

While constituent units with the same constitutional status are the main subnational feature of federations, there are some cases where parts of the national territory are under a distinct constitutional regime. This can be true for national capitals, territories, and aboriginal or tribal areas. In each case, there may be special fiscal arrangements.

Whether a federation's capital city is in a separate federal district (Argentina, Australia, Brazil, India, Malaysia, Mexico, Nigeria, the United States, and Venezuela); is a federal city (Ethiopia, Russia), is a city-state (Austria, Belgium, Germany); or is a municipality within a constituent unit (Canada, Spain, Switzerland), there can be special financial arrangements for the capital. These may recognize the symbolic importance of the capital as a showcase for the country, or simply the extra costs associated with hosting a national government. Federal policy towards national capitals varies greatly. In many cases, the federal government assumes major costs for infrastructure, parks, and cultural institutions, while in others (such as Switzerland) the capital city receives minimal special treatment beyond compensation for such direct costs as enhanced security. For their property in the capital, federal governments may pay taxes to the capital's government, grants in lieu of tax, or nothing at all. In Nigeria, the federal income tax applies only to federal employees and residents of the national capital.

A number of federations also have areas with the status of territories, which typically do not have constitutional autonomy as they are legally subservient to the federal government. These territories can have large areas and small populations (Australia and Canada). In Australia's case, the Commonwealth-grants regime applies to both the states and territories, and includes a calculation of both fiscal capacity and need, which takes account of the high costs of operation in the Northern Territory. In Canada, the equalization regime looks only at fiscal capacity, not need, so a special and much more generous regime has been developed for the three northern territories in order to recognize their special needs.

In both Canada and the United States, there are lands reserved for aboriginal peoples with autonomous governments. Canada has over 600 Indian bands living on reserves, while the United States has a few hundred Native American reservations, the largest of which are greater in area than the smallest states. These communities have legal and fiscal regimes that are distinct from those of the surrounding provinces or states. Federal and provincial taxes normally do not apply to aboriginals for earnings or transactions on their lands. Ultimate title for property rests with the community, and the costs of local government are borne overwhelmingly by federal payments. In many cases, these regimes have proven ill-adapted to promoting economic development, often creating deep dependency syndromes, especially for smaller or more remote communities. In recent years, a variety of new fiscal approaches have been tried by individual communities.

India has six so-called "tribal" states located in its northeast that have special funding arrangements, tribal land protection and other laws. As well, there are tribal districts and regions within some states with particular arrangements around land and other local matters, but not normally including distinctive fiscal regimes.

7.5 Government enterprises

Government-owned corporations engaged in commercial activity have had a major impact on fiscal federalism in some federations.

Federal and constituent-unit governments in many federations have had a large presence in the commercial economy through corporations owned by them. When these corporations have operated in a purely commercial manner, including private borrowing and the payment of taxes (or equivalent), this has had a minimal impact on fiscal federalism. But more often than not, there are special arrangements for these corporations, which can affect fiscal federalism.

- Some public companies are important sources of ongoing revenue for governments. Federal governments may be able to use such arrangements to avoid or limit tax-sharing obligations with the constituent units. Constituent-unit governments, for their part, may use them to enjoy revenues that will not be included in the calculation of their fiscal capacity for purposes of transfers from the federal government. As well, when government-owned corporations are privatized, the proceeds may not count in revenue-sharing arrangements.

- Government-owned companies may be protected from paying corporate income tax or other taxes to the order of government that does not own them, on the grounds that one government cannot tax another: this is the case with large, provincially owned power utilities in Canada. In many cases, government-owned companies are completely outside the corporate tax regime and make other types of payments to the governments that own them.

- Such companies may provide products or services at subsidized or less than market prices, as has been the case for state petroleum companies in Malaysia and Venezuela. Subsidized pricing reduces the revenues available to governments from companies they own; it can also force major expenditure if the subsidized prices are not adjusted to follow the rising cost of imports, such as oil, as has happened in India, Malaysia, and Pakistan. Alternatively, government-owned corporations may use their monopoly to impose higher prices than a competitive market would—which is equivalent to a tax.

- The accounts of government-owned companies can be "off budget" so that their debts are not consolidated with those of the government, thus reducing fiscal transparency and discipline. Such companies may provide payments, easy credit, or loans to the government that owns them, which can undermine efforts at debt management and even bring on a debt crisis. In Brazil, the federal government was forced to intervene in a debt crisis brought on when lending institutions owned by the states provided too much credit to their governments; eventually, this situation led to the privatization of these institutions.

Thus in examining fiscal arrangements in any federation, it is important to look at the extent of public ownership of commercial enterprises and, where it is significant, to consider how such government-owned corporations relate to the fiscal regime. Special arrangements for them can have a major impact on revenue flows to and among governments.

7.6 Corruption

Corruption plagues many countries and undermines economic growth, environmental quality, and human development. It does not appear better or worse in federations. Corruption within a federation can corrode trust between governments and undermine fiscal arrangements. It poses issues about appropriate transparency and accountability arrangements between governments.

Transparency International's annual reports on perceived corruption levels around the world show federal countries to be among both the best and worst performers. Experts have advanced opposing arguments showing why decentralization can lessen corruption or aggravate it, but there is no consensus on whether there is a strong tendency one way or the other.

Corruption is a complex phenomenon that can be deeply rooted in a society and its governance systems. It can be particularly serious when governments have very high resource revenues because voters seem less sensitive to these revenues being captured by corrupt elites than they are in the case of taxes they themselves pay. Competitive party systems can sometimes limit corruption (because opposition parties expose misdeeds), but they can also be part of the problem (because parties divert funds to their members and organizations).

Within federations, corruption can exist at all levels of government. Central governments have access to greater resources, so may have more risk of large-scale corruption. However, regional and local governments can be taken over by corrupt local bosses, who often face weak opposition and have little or no media surveillance. Corruption can undermine trust between governments in a federation: constituent units can suspect the federal government of not fully reporting on revenues that are meant to be shared, while federal governments can be concerned with how transfers' revenues are used or misused.

It appears corruption decreased in many local governments in India during the 1980-90s when the new panchayat system brought three million locally elected politicians into office. The new councils responded to their electorates and increased the accountability and performance of civil servants and teachers at the village level. In short, empowering locally elected governments may reduce corruption in certain cases.

Nigeria has recognized its challenge of corruption, which grew especially under military rule. Certain of the state governments have diverted major resources for corrupt purposes, thus leaving schools, health care, and infrastructure underfunded. The federal Economic and Financial Crimes Commission has exposed many serious cases, some of which have led to the impeachment of state governors; but such operations always face suspicion of a biased approach to enforcement because the commissions may not be wholly independent. Thus, the national assembly and senate have engaged in their own inquiries. While some experts advocate introducing anti-corruption agencies only after the rule of law is more or less secure, the Nigerian experience, despite its flaws, suggests this course may be too cautious.

Efforts to limit corruption succeed best when they address simultaneously the needs for the rule of law, an independent media, public participation, professional bureaucracies and courts, and transparency and accountability. As well, countries providing foreign investment have a responsibility to police nationals who may offer bribes in foreign countries. While the risk of corruption is strongly related to the level of human and economic development as well as resource wealth, all countries can take measures to improve their performance.

A major problem in confronting corruption in government is creating credible checks and balances. Federal systems may have a potential advantage here, though they have not really exploited it to date. Where a federal government provides large transfers or shared revenues to the constituent units, it has a natural interest in the probity with which these funds are used. The constituent units, for their part, have an interest in transparency at the federal level, at least in relation to revenues that must be shared. So if autonomous oversight mechanisms within each order of government are weak, perhaps there is room for each order of government to have some formal oversight over the other.

Conclusion

This little book has provided a brief overview of fiscal federalism. The subject is both political and economic. It is political in that money is a type of power: how it is raised and used is intimately linked to the decision-making structure and political dynamics of a federation. It is economic in that the management of divided sovereignty in such matters as taxation, government spending, and regulation can have a substantial impact on the functioning and stability of an economy, its efficiency, and its sharing of wealth.

We have looked at the allocation of expenditure responsibilities, the structure of tax regimes, the allocation of specific tax and revenue sources, the sharing and transfer of revenues between federal, constituent-unit, and municipal governments, and some aspects of broader economic management and institutional arrangements in federations. In all these matters, there is a tremendous variation in practice among federal countries. The variety of arrangements reflects the very different histories and characters of federations. There is no single best way to manage things and each country must find its own solutions.

That said, we can learn much from the study of fiscal federalism. The subject provides us with analytical tools and evaluative criteria that aid understanding and critical judgments. The different experiences of federations can provide both inspiration from their creativity and cautionary tales from their mistakes.

It is hoped that this introductory overview has given the reader a sense of the range and nature of issues in fiscal federalism, and insights into how to think critically about them.

Further Readings

Fiscal federalism has a rich practical, theoretical, and comparative literature. The following are a few important and largely current selections.

Ahmad, Ehtisham and Georgio Brosio, eds. *Handbook of Fiscal Federalism*. Northampton, MA: Edward Elgar, 2006.

Bird, Richard and Robert Ebel, eds. *Fiscal Fragmentation in Decentralized Countries: Subsidiarity, Solidarity and Asymmetry*. Northampton, MA: World Bank, 2007.

Bird, Richard and François Vaillancourt, eds. *Fiscal Decentralization in Developing Countries*. Cambridge: Cambridge University Press, 1998.

Boadway, Robin and Anwar Shah. *Fiscal Federalism: Principles and Practice of Multi-Order Governance*. New York: Cambridge University Press, 2009.

Boadway, Robin and Anwar Shah, eds. *Intergovernmental Fiscal Transfers: Principles and Practice*. Washington, DC: World Bank, 2007.

Bosch, Nuria and José M. Duran, eds. *Fiscal Federalism and Political Decentralization: Lessons from Spain, Germany and Canada*. Northhampton, MA: Edward Elgar, 2008.

Imbeau, Louis M. and François Petry, eds. *Fiscal Federalism in Theory and Practice*. Lanham, ML: Lexington Books, 2004.

Oates, Wallace. "Towards a second-generation theory of fiscal federalism." *International Tax and Public Finance* 12 (2005).

Oates, Wallace. "An essay on fiscal federalism." *Journal of Economic Literature* 37 (1999).

Rodden, Jonathan. *Hamilton's Paradox: Promise and Perils of Fiscal Federalism*. New York: Cambridge University Press, 2006.

Rodden, Jonathan, Gunnar Eskeland, and Jennie Litvak, eds. *Fiscal Decentralization and the Challenge of Hard Budget Constraints.* Cambridge, MA: MIT Press, 2003.

Shah, Anwar, ed. *The Practice of Fiscal Federalism: Comparative Perspectives.* Montreal: McGill-Queen's University Press, 2007.

Ter-Minassian, Teresa, ed. *Fiscal Federalism in Theory and Practice.* Washington, DC: International Monetary Fund, 1997.

Treisman, Daniel. *The Architecture of Government: Rethinking Political Decentralization.* Cambridge: Cambridge University Press, 2007.

Wallack, Jessica S. and T.N. Srinivasan, eds. *Federalism and Economic Reform.* Cambridge: Cambridge University Press, 2006.

Watts, Ronald L. *Comparing Federal Systems,* 3rd ed. Montreal: McGill-Queen's University Press, 2008.

Watts, Ronald. *The Spending Power in Federal Systems: A Comparative Study.* Kingston, ON: Institute of Intergovernmental Relations, 1999.

Watts, Ronald L., and Rupak Chattopadhyay, eds. *Emerging Issues in Fiscal Federalism.* New Delhi Viva Books and Forum of Federations, 2008.

Useful websites

"The Federalism Library," online: *Forum of Federations,* http://www.forumfed.org/en/federalism/library.php.

"Fiscal Federalism," online: *Institute for Public Economics,* University of Alberta, http://www.uofaweb.ualberta.ca/ipe/federalism.cfm.

"OECD Fiscal Federalism Network," online: OECD, http://www.oecd.org/department/0,3355,en_2649_35929024_1_1_1_1_1,00.html.

Publications

Federations, http://www.forumfed.org/en/products/federations.php.

Publius: The Journal of Federalism, http://publius.oxfordjournals.org.

Index